# CHIEF
## OF STAFF

Salaita, Chris Sanders, Brian Screnar, Kirsten Smith, Fraser Stark, Ben Stephens, Lennart Streibel, Magda Swanson, Andrea Voytko, Adam Vraves, Yvette Wagner, Rick Waldron, Melanie Willis, Mette Wind Meyhoff, Mark Wooley, Tachi Yamada.

I am just as deeply grateful to those who chose to remain anonymous and did not want to be named here.

I first envisioned researching and writing a book of this nature while sitting in front of a computer screen. I did not anticipate the coffees, happy hours and dinners, cab rides, and walks around Green Lake in Seattle with people who would shape this content and challenge me to think about it in new ways. Thanks, Shelby Barnes, for asking powerful questions on those walks around Green Lake; Charles Bicknell, for your thoughts on the role in insurance; Guy Ellis and Claudia Myers, for so many conversations about our work together and the book; Kristi James, for never letting me stop at the superficial level; Lori Hargrave, for your inquiry on the role at IV (it really got me thinking about the distinguishing characteristics); Anne O'Donnell, for keeping me focused on what I could get traction with (when I wanted to tell so many stories with all the data!); Bryce Olson, for asking me some simple and powerful questions about the organization of chapters; Sandy Smith, for your questions and ideas during that Santa Barbara cab ride to Hudson and your willingness to connect me to people you know; Will Maroon, Jennifer Yu, Peter Raven, and Greg Scully at the Seattle University International Consulting Course program for your research; and Adam Wilson, for goading me into finally getting a Twitter account. Additional thanks to Matt Dunn, Marc Kuyper, Greg and Jackie Lang, Jon Osterberg, Galand Marshall, Sean Neely, Jesse Rice, and Hank Wysong for your moral support and encouragement.

Thank you to my beloved wife, Katie, who has sacrificed her kitchen table and put up with my clutter (and angst, and celebration) for the last year or so as I focused on this project.

Ultimately, I thank God for this opportunity and the experiences that have led up to it. What a challenge and growth experience this has been!

# INTRODUCTION

## The $50 Million Question

In a meeting, the president of a high-tech company wants to know how her executive leadership team plan to secure a good return from a series of potential deals that just came into the sales pipeline. Although these deals are not the company's only revenue source, they would help the leadership team hit their collective revenue targets, and the company's board have made clear their desire for the team to execute well on turning this opportunity into a win for the company and its investors. In the meeting, the head of sales offers, "My team members say that they have line of sight to $50–$100 million in revenue this year alone, from multiple deals." After a moment's pause, the president responds, "Okay. Then by next week I want to see a concrete plan that gets us to $100 million." The sales head agrees. "I'll take care of it right away," he says. The chief of staff, who until now has been silently watching the discussion unfold, noting the nonverbal cues around the room and glancing at the clock, jumps in. "Wait. I heard you say $50–100 million, not just $100 million. I think we should find out if 50 or 100 is the more realistic number. If we just create a goal around $100 million and the team can only support $50 million realistically, we set false expectations with the board, internal teams, and potentially investors that could come back to bite us later. Can we use the range for planning or go with the lower number?"

It seems like a simple question. Yet nobody else asks it. The chief of staff is relying on over a year of working with this leadership team, his sense of the particular quirks of each of its leaders, and a history of learning experiences that predate the president and several leadership team members. He also knows that his boss—the president—is set on a plan for $100 million because of pressure from the board to hit revenue numbers, and last year wasn't as strong as previous years. The gravity of getting such a decision right fills the room today. If this group sets the wrong expectations, the board is likely to reject any of the potential deals that come in at less than the top figure, even if they are "pretty good." They will hold out for the bird in the bush rather than the two in hand. They will do this because their trusted leadership team told the board after today's meeting that it was worth more.

It's only dramatizing a little to say that the chief of staff asked a $50 million question. And the stakes are higher than money. Other risks include the credibility of the president and the leadership team, and at least some of the trust that has been built up and down the organization over the past couple years since the president and several executives came on board. A miscue here could tempt the board to jump in and micromanage or rescue. Someone who has spent years building a pretty good career could find his or her job and individual reputation on the line. Everyone else in the room—the staff VPs and even the president herself—has a positional point of view or a personal agenda, and possibly political pressures that make it difficult to ask a question like this. Everyone's moving fast. Each person around the table hears something different, even though only one person has spoken. With stakes this high, the president sleeps a little better knowing someone will ask these questions if she misses them and that someone has her back and the back of her leadership team. That's why she has a chief of staff.

## My Experience

I first stepped into the office of the president and chief operating officer of Intellectual Ventures in the middle of 2011, as a newly minted chief of staff. From that moment, I experienced a faster pace and higher stakes in my communications, discussions, and decision making than I had known previously. I shifted from coordinating work at a tactical, peer level in a sales operations role to more strategic duties, like setting business rhythms for board and executive team meetings, setting the framework for the company's annual planning process, and handling new tactical duties like running air traffic control for most of the requests for the president's time. My perspective quickly broadened as I met leaders from all corners of the business that I'd previously had little need to know (or access to); as I learned the goals and concerns of those leaders; and as I witnessed team dynamics that I had previously only seen from a distance or heard rumors of. I learned to what degree the rumors and legends I had heard among the rank-and-file actually resembled the reality of the history and decision-making processes at the top levels of the company.

I relied on my predecessor for as many tips and tricks as he could provide. Yet our plan for an overlapping transition period of two or three weeks was superseded by his already being caught up in the demands of the role he was transitioning to. We got a couple of hours together in the first few weeks. I learned about some of my new responsibilities only after a deadline was missed or a meeting was missing important attendees. In those moments, my gut reaction and temptation was to point fingers, to lay blame on my predecessor or our less-than-ideal handoff. But I quickly learned that nobody else cared. It was my job now. So I decided to own it and drive it, with all its good and bad. I relied on the business experience and relational abilities that had led me to being accepted for this role and chose to respond as if I were on an epic adventure.

I mostly figured the role out on my own, through experience. I couldn't find many resources for this somewhat unique position and its particular challenges. No training. No how-to manual. No framework for thinking about the role. No template to plug in and start from. My performance reviews went well, and I felt successful in the role. On the other hand, I sensed that I could have done even more during my time in the role had I been able to reference a body of knowledge or best practices from those who had gone before me. As I inquired more broadly of other chiefs of staff, I found that their experience was similar to mine. One chief of staff said, "There's a lot of confusion about the role, because most people's experience is high-level news articles or watching [the television show] *The West Wing*. The chief of staff in business doesn't have an anchor. No common base of reference." Former Ernst & Young chief of staff Chris Sanders says, "A Google search turns up info on the government, medical, and some IT versions of the role—it's why I started a LinkedIn group for Corporate Chiefs of Staff." As a former technical and creative writer turned business leader, I looked for an opportunity to do the research, to pull together the body of knowledge and best practices.

## My Research

My research began with the gaps in the existing literature. Volumes have been written about the chief of staff in American politics—*Chief of Staff*, by Mark Vertreese; *The Nerve Center*, by Joseph V. Hughes Jr. and Holly O. Hughes; and *Chief of Staff, Vol. 1*, by Major General David T. Zabecki are popular examples. The political chief of staff has even been glorified in television shows like *The West Wing*, *Commander in Chief*, *House of Cards*, *Scandal*, *Veep*, a segment of *60 Minutes*, and *The Gatekeepers*; and in movies like *Swimming with Sharks* and *Thirteen Days*. About 40 percent of my interview respondents said they learned tips and tricks watching *The West Wing*. There is also ample literature on the medical chief of staff in various industry-specific publications in the United States, like "Surfing the Waves of Credentialing" or state-by-state manuals defining hospital governing boards, of which a chief of staff is normally a part (see the Washington State Hospital Association's *Governing Board Manual, 2006*, as an example).

Yet little has been written about the application of the chief of staff role to business. A number of articles and blog posts over the past couple years indicate that the role has gained some level of prominence. See "Latest CEO Accessory: A Chief of Staff," by

Beth Kowitt with Alyssa Abkowitz;[1] and "Chiefs of Staff Make Their Way to Corporate America," by Brooke Sopelsa.[2] Patricia Seemann, CEO and Founder of The 3am Group, wrote a paper called *Need a Chief of Staff?* that she makes available upon request to her clients. There is at least one critique of the role: "Check with My Chief of Staff," by Jon Picoult.[3] Mostly, these are high-level catalogs of some of the role's job functions, interspersed with examples of the use of the role by some of the biggest names in business: Goldman Sachs, AOL, ING, Aflac, Yahoo!, Polo Ralph Lauren.

Al Chase of White Rhino Partners wrote a white paper that I believe is the deepest and most comprehensive look at the role in business prior to the publication of this book, in *Chief of Staff—A Force Multiplier!*[4] In his paper, Chase outlines some of the reasons executives gravitate to the role and what kind of skills and experience successful chiefs of staff bring to the table. And the white paper meets a need for this audience, because it receives thousands of views per month, and he has updated it several times since its original publication in 2006.

Even with these notable contributions, I could not find any of the following in the existing literature:

- An assessment of both the general business environment that has led to the role's use in corporate settings and the specific organizational dynamics that tend to lend themselves to a successful chief of staff role.
- A deep look at the perceived benefits to the supported executive, other leaders in the organization, and the organization as a whole, of having a chief of staff.
- Once the decision has been made to hire a chief of staff, the subtleties and nuances of finding and hiring the right people.
- Common pitfalls and best practices for the CEO getting the most out of the role and for managing the integration of a chief of staff with the CEO's direct reports, especially in the early going but also with regard to ongoing management issues that frequently arise.

- Best practices for evolving the role over time.
- The most common traits and characteristics of successful chiefs of staff. For example, although much of the literature contained high-level lists of competencies like "communication" and "leadership," I wanted to find out what these looked like *in this role*, as well as whether there were certain personality traits that successful chiefs of staff exhibited.

Starting with those gaps in the current literature, I set out to interview as many chiefs of staff, C-suite executives, and HR executives as I could about their experience in or with the role. In the end, I interviewed more than 60 of them around the globe, from small- to medium-size companies like Intellectual Ventures, Emaar (United Arab Emirates), Mahindra GenZ, and SCYNEXIS, to venerable giants like Advance Micro Devices (AMD), Banamex, Barclays, Boeing, Cisco, Direct Line Insurance, eBay, Ericsson, Ernst & Young, Flextronics, Intel, Microsoft, Pacific Gas and Electric Company, PayPal, Providence Health & Services, and Wells Fargo. I even interviewed board members, executives who did not use a chief of staff, as well as a few executive assistants, as points of context and comparison.

I partnered with a team of Seattle University students to gather demographic, salary, and career progression data from a broad range of available sources. I worked with colleagues Colleen Hunter and Vivian Mason at Slalom Consulting to articulate and connect the leader's position (Chapter 2) with common deliverables (Chapter 4) and competencies (Chapter 5). I reviewed more than 80 secondary sources, such as articles, studies, and books. Finally, as work on this book gained steam, I began consulting on chief of staff issues and began a chief of staff peer group for corporate, nonprofit, academic, and political chiefs of staff in and around Seattle, where I gained additional insights into what boards of directors and CEOs are looking for and what chiefs of staff commonly experience.

This book took shape from the patterns and trends that emerged out of these piles of data and information.

**Written for the C-Suite and Board of Directors, Applicable to Many**

Although I am ultimately writing this book for senior executives (CEOs and board members) who have decisions to make about creating or evolving a chief of staff role, I have written it in such a way that it will be useful to other leaders who use chiefs of staff or quasi-chiefs of staff, incumbent chiefs of staff, HR executives, and even prospective chiefs of staff or people who are curious about how a role like this can benefit their careers.

Other important audiences who should be able to directly apply insight from this book are these:

- Midlevel professionals in an organization looking for a shortcut to the executive ranks
- Senior-level leaders in an organization who have determined they are not reaching the organization's top leadership spot but still have a lot of experience and company/industry knowledge to offer, similar to the elder statesman in politics
- Current or former chiefs of staff in politics or the military who are looking for a transition to the corporate sector
- Venture capitalists who are looking for creative solutions to operational challenges in rapidly growing startup organizations
- Individuals who have taken time off from work for various reasons and are looking for a way to re-enter the corporate world
- Experienced consultants who are looking for a transition to a product company
- Executive assistants who are looking for ways to better work with a chief of staff in their office or who want to step into broader leadership roles beyond the EA role
- CFOs who need to justify the return on investment of a chief of staff position to a board
- Coaches or consultants who work regularly and directly with senior executives and/or their chiefs of staff

My hope is that after reading this book you will have a thorough framework for deciding if and how the chief of staff role can serve your organization, how you should hire for it, and how you can get the most out of the role and manage the person in it for his or her future success.

# SO, YOU THINK YOU NEED A CHIEF OF STAFF?

**1**

# Definition, History, and Corporate Context of the Chief of Staff Role

Frequently, senior leaders of companies hear from their peer network about how a chief of staff can be helpful in managing their affairs, or they read one of the several articles online about how a chief of staff is helping a prominent senior leader at another organization. I have interviewed more than 60 chiefs of staff, C-suite executives, and HR executives in various industries and around the globe on the chief of staff role in business. One thing is clear: the decision to create a chief of staff role is not to be taken lightly. If the role is carelessly crafted and executed, the chief of staff can be seen as a wedge between you and your organization, an unnecessary layer of bureaucracy, and a complete waste of resources.

About a quarter of respondents said that when the chief of staff role was created in their organizations, the supported executives knew that they needed help but weren't quite sure how to articulate the nature of that help. In many situations, they were responding somewhere in between. Because of this variety, HR executives in my interviews reported having a hard time benchmarking the role.

Still, there are some core characteristics that tend to define a chief of staff. A chief of staff is someone who does the following:

- Uses organization skills to manage a portfolio of projects for the CEO.
- Helps the staff and their teams interpret, understand, and carry out the CEO's vision and strategic intent.
- Helps a CEO prioritize projects and business impacts so that the CEO and his or her direct reports are moving forward with only the most important work.
- Exercises exceptional discretion with confidential information to keep the CEO apprised of what's going on in the organization and, where possible, to keep the organization informed of what's going on at the top.
- Manages business rhythms such as recurrent leadership meetings and governance processes on behalf of the CEO.
- Provides analysis, recommendations, and options to the CEO regarding decisions to be made or problems to be solved in internal or external meetings.
- Attends and facilitates complex, cross-departmental discussions to ensure that good decisions are reached (versus so-called yes-people simply agreeing with the CEO) and that decisions are carried out.
- Acts as proxy and information funnel, filter, and facilitator for the CEO, dealing with as many issues as possible before they reach the CEO's desk, representing the CEO's point of view, and making decisions, as needed, in the executive's absence.
- Serves as thought partner and coach to the CEO, influencing the overall agenda for the organization, offering the CEO and his or her direct reports perspectives they might not see, uncovering or helping the team uncover new possibilities, and challenging ideas before they are committed to action.

- Manages risk by bridging interdepartmental gaps, by connecting the executive to what is really going on in the organization, by keeping shop while the executive is away, by maintaining continuity during leadership changes, and, in early-stage companies, by being the negative feedback loop for behaviors that don't meet long-term growth objectives.
- Manages a strategic planning and budgeting process for the executive's organization.
- Manages or helps manage the executive's communications, brand, and relationships in the organization.
- Might or might not manage a departmental budget or have direct reports.
- Accomplishes all of the above by using a combination of soft skills, primarily managed-ego or servant leadership, political savvy, exceptional tact and discretion with confidential information, a learning orientation, a balance of organization skills and flexibility, the ability to connect dots between seemingly disparate activities or teams in the organization, and coaching.

Several leaders I interviewed referred to Radar O'Reilly from the classic television show *M\*A\*S\*H*. Radar is a character who seems to have a sixth sense about the organization, who can finish his boss's sentences, and who can not only anticipate organizational needs before they happen (he is often the first to hear medevac helicopters approaching the field hospital where the show is set) but also uses a keen resourcefulness to obtain supplies—seemingly out of nowhere—that the camp needs.

## WHERE DID THE CHIEF OF STAFF ROLE COME FROM?

Although I primarily seek to address the chief of staff in *business* with this book, it can be helpful to look briefly at the historical context of the role to better understand how it fits in a corporate context. Although arguably every government or military leader in history has had advisors, I have found two historical threads from which all formal chief of staff roles seem to originate. The Japanese government created the role of Lord Keeper of the Privy Seal as early as 699, and it appears to have remained the same in structure and purpose in Japan until it was abolished in 1945.[1] The Carolingian monarchy created the Lord Chancellor as the keeper of the national seal of England around 1066 and the Lord Privy Seal as the keeper of the king's or queen's personal seal in 1307, even though some versions of the role might have existed, informally, earlier. Following these two threads, the French aide de camp appears to have come into being around 1665, when Philippe de Courcillon became a colonel in King Louis the XIV's regiment and served as an aide de camp until he became a provincial governor in 1667.[2]

To study the precise evolution of these roles, within their particular contexts, over time, is beyond the scope of this book, but with their proximity to heads of state and with their delegated authority, the individuals who held all of these behind-the-scenes staff roles wielded tremendous power and influence from the top down and from the bottom up. Here are some famous examples and brief descriptions of their power and influence:

- Richard Neville, the 16th Earl of Warwick, who unseated two English kings while serving as their chief advisors and directly influenced the outcome of the War of the Roses and the future of the English monarchy.[3]
- Thomas More (Lord Chancellor) and Thomas Cromwell (Lord Privy Seal and holder of multiple other titles and seats on the Privy Council), who are widely regarded as the brains behind Henry VIII's hot-headed reign, securing the crown's power in a tumultuous time and ushering in the English Reformation.[4]
- General Count Philip de Ségur, whose involvement in some of Napoleon's major battles, as military aide de camp and diplomat, helped secure France's dominant position in European politics in the early 1800s.[5]

- Makino Nobuaki, who advised Emperor Shōwa (Hirohito) on improving Anglo-Japanese and Japanese-American relations, even at risk to his own life from the militarists who opposed him and tried to assassinate him. He continued to advise the emperor after the end of World War II.[6]

As a quick aside, an astute observer of history might note that these historical references include some infamous examples of leaders being betrayed by their trusted advisors. Such an observer would be right. The Earl of Warwick unseated two kings while serving as their chief advisor during the War of the Roses, largely in support of his own ego and the ambitions of a class of English nobles. His actions give rise to a legitimate, if Machiavellian, line of questioning: Can a chief of staff's familiarity with your strengths and vulnerabilities, over time, increase the chances of your being betrayed? It seems theoretically possible. I don't have conclusive data to answer this question. The closest modern example of such betrayal that I could find, at the top of a business, however, was Wes Yoder. Yoder was founder and CEO of a faith-based literary agency and speakers bureau, who handled such talents as Amy Grant and the best-selling title *The Purpose-Driven Life*, and who faced bankruptcy after he entrusted a chief operating officer and a vice president with many of his day-to-day responsibilities.[7]

The prospect of betrayal is probably a greater risk if you have a very senior and sophisticated advisor (VP level or higher), who could be in your line of succession or who could be aligned very closely with someone in your line of succession, and therefore would have motive for undermining you. Individuals in such a position could—intentionally or unintentionally—second-guess and undermine your efforts as a way to better position themselves or the other in your line of succession. Although some caution is always advisable, most of the people I interviewed simply did not experience or see the potential for this extreme scenario of betrayal playing out.

Al Chase posits that the chief of staff role jumped from the military to business with retiring military officers entering the business world after having served a term as chief of staff, aide de camp,

## WHY AND HOW SHOULD I THINK ABOUT THE CHIEF OF STAFF IN MY CONTEMPORARY CONTEXT?

Running a business is far more complex than it was just a few decades ago. Given the increasingly rapid pace of technological change, globalization, the regulatory landscape, and the fact that CEOs cite complexity as their number-one concern,[11] many leaders have found the chief of staff to be a useful and versatile tool to help deal with this complexity. Some boards of directors have influenced the decision to hire one or more chiefs of staff in the C-suite to manage the risks associated with complexity. In fact, as of this publication, I could identify 68,000 people worldwide with "chief of staff" in their title, minus military branches or government affiliations.

If you are an executive thinking about creating a chief of staff role, understanding some historical trends and your position in that historical context of business leadership might help you decide whether the chief of staff is right for your organization. Your incumbent chief of staff or candidate for the role must also understand your context in a broader business landscape in order to fully appreciate how he or she can be most useful.

### Growing complexities of running a business

If you literally drew the changes in executive life over the past 50 years, you might embody them by drawing two cartoon people. The first, shown in Figure 1.2, would be a white executive cartoon guy with a number of attributes to his side: leads the company he "grew up" in; works 9 to 6; focuses on product development, marketing, and sales against known competitors; chiefly targets the local market (U.S. companies in the United States, European companies in Europe, etc.); enjoys operation relatively unencumbered by government oversight or intervention, even though he would complain loudly about the unprecedented level of regulation he faces; spends a lot of time wining and dining potential customers at his own home. There are probably other attributes, but this depiction would be a good starting point.

FIGURE 1.2    Senior Leader/Executive 50 Years Ago

*Leads the company he "grew up" in*

*A primary responsibility is wining and dining clients*

*Typical day: 9am–6pm*

*Local workforce*

*Grouses about unprecedented regulation, but actual regulation is relatively low*

*Relatively stable markets, known competitors*

The other cartoon person, shown in Figure 1.3, would be a woman, or maybe a dark-skinned person of either gender, or maybe even a 25-year-old; a more contemporary face of the corporate executive. And out to her side would be a different set of attributes: leads different companies, even different industries than where her career began; must be available or on-call 24/7; competes with other companies, increasing pace of technological change, geo-political trends, and government regulations (tax and finance, environmental, employment/labor); operates globally; manages not just substantive business numbers like profits and costs but also IT, people, personal brand, and public relations issues that shift with social media trends; travels internationally; and manages diverse teams globally.

These are fundamentally two different types of people with different skills and experiences that contribute to their success. Executives have always been busy. And, presumably, they've always felt the weight of their constituencies on their shoulders.[12] Still, while some aspects of being an executive might not have changed much over the years, a lot is different.[13] My interview respondents agree that the most important changes are the increasingly rapid

**FIGURE 1.3**   Senior Leader/Executive Today

pace of technological change, globalization, and policy and regulatory changes.

## The increasingly rapid pace of technological change

If you thought it was tough being longtime General Motors head Alfred P. Sloan, worrying about staying on top of an industry in the 1940s in a game where it took decades for industry leaders to shift,[14] try being at the helm of today's tech giants, where leaders change more frequently and disruption is more common than stability. The pace of technological change affects the products you make; how you make, distribute, market, and sell them; how you operate internally; and how you respond to public sentiment. Technological changes and related trends like mass air travel, video conferencing, smartphones, and online collaboration tools increase the expectations for an always-on, highly responsive workforce and senior leaders. The amount of data that is available, in real time, dwarfs the amounts previously available, and making useful information, not to mention decisions, out of those mountains of data takes time.

## Globalization

Globalization makes life uniquely complicated for today's business leaders by changing the face of the workforce and by shifting trends in international politics and policies that influence or control business outcomes.[15] Today's C-level executive will likely lead some form of globally distributed team of unprecedented cultural and racial diversity, and will need to keep a keen eye on the flux of world powers and their alliances because of the many ramifications for energy policy, foreign policy, labor availability and costs, market volatility, and trade routes. Finally, that executive will have to have a much more nuanced understanding of geo-political trends, in more locales, and how they affect manufacturing, logistics, and distribution and supply chains, than his or her predecessors.

## Policy and regulation

My purpose here is not to argue that the general regulatory environment is too heavy or too light, but rather that senior leaders, at least in some geo-political contexts, need to think about policy, regulation, and the influence of consumers to affect these, to an unprecedented degree. It is simply a fact that the sheer numbers of laws and regulations on the books tend to grow faster than they contract. Plus, the behaviors of some bad actors around the world (Enron, Worldcom, a host of subprime lenders and derivatives traders globally) have led to an increase in regulation or oversight in some countries and in some industries, with C-suite executives assuming fail-and-go-to-jail responsibility for noncompliance. Globally (at least in Western contexts), the body of case law has grown steadily in the areas of hiring and firing; wages and hours; contractors and vendors; discrimination and harassment; leave and time off; the digital age's effects on privacy rights in the workplace and corporate liability; and health and safety. Many of the technological changes I referred to earlier provide consumers an unprecedented way to offer feedback not just on products (reviews, for example) but also on corporate practices (by mobilizing events, boycotts, and online petitions, for example).

## General complexity

Outside of my interviews, ample evidence in the literature addresses the increasing complexity—and the consequences of not dealing with it—in the C-suite. Existing business literature highlights the challenges faced by C-level executives, who are hiring chief strategy officers, chief customer officers, and other nontraditional C-suite roles, to help them manage the complexity.[16] For example, in "The New Path to the C-Suite," Boris Groysberg, L. Kevin Kelly, and Bryan MacDonald highlight other changes to the roles of C-level executives as well:

> One strikingly consistent finding: Once people reach the C-suite, technical and functional expertise matters less than leadership skills and a strong grasp of business fundamentals. Chief information officers need to know how to create business models; chief financial officers, how to develop risk management strategies; chief human resource officers, how to design a succession plan and a talent structure that will provide a competitive edge. In other words, the skills that help you climb to the top won't suffice once you get there. We're beginning to see C-level executives who have more in common with their executive peers than they do with the people in the functions they run. And today members of senior management are expected not only to support the CEO on business strategies but also to offer their own insights and contribute to key decisions.[17]

Brett Thomas writes on his Integral Leadership Manifesto site:

It doesn't require much imagination to recognize the complexity of problems (and conditions, worldviews, worker types, etc.) that leaders face today. In fact, the term "complexity" is being used increasingly in boardrooms and in publications read by leaders. A 2010 study of global CEOs conducted by IBM in 2010 is particularly insightful. It lists complexity as the #1 concern of global CEOs.[18]

---

## UNIVERSAL COMPETENCIES

### Systems and process thinking

I describe the systems and process thinking competency in the section on "Universal Competencies" in Chapter 5. Additional insights from my interviews include these:

- A chief of staff must always have the context in mind. This can mean the general business environment in which the company operates or the knowledge that a change in one area can have ripple effects throughout the organization. As Julius Sinkevicius, a longtime Microsoft chief of staff, says, "If content is king, context is a god."

- The chief of staff must excel at connecting the dots between efforts in multiple departments or between seemingly unrelated work streams.

Another high-tech chief of staff says, "You have to constantly ground everyone—even your executive—in the overall goals of what you're trying to accomplish. People lose sight of that when they're doing the tactical work."

One former chief of staff says, "There's no way to train someone to connect dots in the organization. They have to know what's going on in multiple parts of the business, understand the tribal knowledge, have a point of view on everything [known] that comes across the executive's desk, and be able to tell people, 'I see what you're trying to do, but I'm concerned because of the potential impact to x in another part of the organization.'"

---

A study by the Center for Creative Leadership describes the changes in the structure of organizational leadership in recent decades: "[I]n the last decade, we've seen a rise in the use of senior teams for top leadership as the complexity resulting from globalization, increased diversity in both the marketplace and the organization, and similar factors has increased."[19]

The consequences of not managing complexity well can be severe.[20] For example, although the numbers have leveled a bit in recent years, CEO dismissals increased by 170 percent from 1995

"Not all VPs have a chief of staff, but some do. It all depends on the business need for that leader and their organization." These companies, and the divisions within them, can be either in rapid growth, incremental growth, or a period of relative stability.

Some leaders had strong opinions that the chief of staff role makes more sense during a period of rapid growth, when change and complexity are rampant and likely to challenge any CEO's ability to keep up. Likening his organization to homeostasis in biology, one executive said that in the early days, when there are fewer written rules and policies, there is room in the organization for terrific creativity, flexibility, and adaptability. There is also more room for duplication of effort in different parts of the business, ambiguous role definition that leaves important work undone because nobody thought it was their job, and room for bad actors to run afoul of commonly accepted social or business norms—even laws. The chief of staff, in this situation, serves as the negative feedback loop that corrects such behaviors or keeps them from undermining the broader organization's long-term objectives. In this instance, the chief of staff is a bringer of stability to the early, relative chaos of an organization's life.

Others argued that it is precisely when growth slows, when an organization has shifted from a few people performing multiple roles to a larger company requiring more focused and specialized expertise that the chief of staff can add the most value. Some included regulated industries in this category. In this instance, the chief of staff is program manager, probably leaning on past project-management acumen to bring efficiency to larger groups of people, adding process and standardization—or at least guiding principles that other teams could build process and standards around—and enforcing governance and compliance with internal or external policies.

The range of opinions on size and growth indicate that the chief of staff can be helpful in many stages of a company's evolution, but with different emphasis, or emphases, in each stage. See Chapter 5, "Finding and Hiring the Right Candidates," for more detail on these emphases.

## SIGNIFICANT CHANGES IN LEADERSHIP OR ORGANIZATION STRUCTURE

Organizations experiencing significant leadership change might be good candidates for a chief of staff. These changes could include a high turnover in the CEO's office or a high turnover in executive staff under a CEO.

Many top leaders (VPs and higher) at large companies go on to C-level positions elsewhere in industry. From a talent development point of view, some would say that the greater the turnover in top leaders, the greater the potential to circulate new chiefs of staff into the role with the flux of leaders. From a business continuity standpoint, others would say that the greater the turnover, the greater the need for stability, continuity, and knowledge management in the chief of staff role. Both are right

The chief of staff can maintain a constant rhythm or continuous thread during these changes, especially in managing relationships with external parties like investors, the press, and customers, whose continued good relationships are not just desired but critical for the organization to reach short-term or long-term goals. When the executive at the head of an organization departs, or a new one is inbound, there is always an adjustment to be made by many people:

- The executive
- The chief of staff
- The staff
- The broader organization
- Customers
- Investors
- Press contacts

Adjustments can involve scheduling and pace, behavioral patterns, interpersonal dynamics, team cohesion, performance levels, motivations, and the confidence of the broader organization in leadership. People are taking cues from the new leader to see how things will play out, and if they had a long-standing relationship with the old executive, they will be starting from scratch. For example, imagine you're the head of baseball scouting for the Oakland A's when Sandy Alderson and Billy Beane implement sabermetrics as the basis of scouting. It's a whole new world for you and your organization. If the leader is promoted from within the organization, he has the unenviable task of managing the ensuing conflicts that arise out of social biases and previous relationships between the executive and the staff. The new leader may struggle with conflicting emotions or competing commitments around having authority over people he was just peers with yesterday. Or he or she might have made plans and promises that can no longer be achieved because of the changed dynamic.

The career chief of staff model is best suited for this kind of transition, although I have seen instances of the rotational chief of staff model handling its fair share of change. As one example, Melanie Willis served as the chief of staff to three consecutive executives in seven months during the final assembly of a major commercial airliner. Her presence helped keep a constant thread amidst the turnover, minimizing "churn." People knew who to go to for their questions, despite changes in the ultimate decision makers.

I treat the talent development aspect of this dynamic separately in the section on "Competitive Advantage Through Talent Development and Succession Plans," later in this chapter.

## MULTIPLE, DIVERSE LINES OF BUSINESS (INCLUDING CONSOLIDATION)

A company that is launching new product lines from within itself, consolidating internal divisions, merging with another company, or absorbing an acquired company, generally experiences, at least temporarily, a period of increased complexity that a chief of staff can help with. Managing the many moving operational pieces of efforts like these and coordinating, engaging, and coaching the staff-level leaders through the long-term changes that are required can demand time and attention that you simply don't have. In this situation, a chief of staff can use his or her breadth and depth of existing networks in the organization(s) to stay abreast of what's going on, to fact-check data and reports coming to you from the various departments, to help resolve the cross-departmental conflicts that invariably arise, and to deal with other day-to-day issues so that you can stay focused on the big picture.

A great example is the way Diana Deen helped Barry Koch sort and prioritize issues coming across his desk as their company, Washington Mutual, was acquired by JP Morgan Chase & Co. in the wake of the 2008 US financial crisis and Koch became tasked with partnering with his counterpart at JPMorgan Chase to ensure that both organizations remained in line with regulatory compliance throughout the merger. There were so many tasks coming so suddenly from so many directions that prioritizing and managing them became a major challenge. Deen's first order of business was to reduce the sheer number of items that bubbled up to Koch's level by delegating, dealing with them at her level, or deferring them. She also brought on new IT tools to manage a backlog of compliance issues at Washington Mutual and managed the off-boarding of 500+ consultants. Finally, she helped Koch integrate his vision and agenda into the larger JP Morgan Chase formal strategic plan that met with ultimate approval by their chief compliance officer and general counsel.

As another example, healthcare providers in the United States had been consolidating for years when a combination of the 2008 recession and passage of the Affordable Care Act accelerated the consolidations. As providers found themselves getting paid less each year, per client, to provide healthcare, they found other ways to maintain revenue. John Fletcher, who served in at least two corporate chief of staff roles for Providence Health & Services says, "Consolidation generally happened so that providers could centralize services, find savings in the supply chain, and improve their debt financing." While he was regional chief executive for Providence, Providence acquired the Swedish Healthcare System, and Fletcher was tapped for a vice president–level role that functioned as a chief of staff for the leadership of the newly combined organizations. He says, "A lot of healthcare systems use a director of integration or integration officer like me, and they go away after about three to five years." In that role, he was responsible for the integration of several departments, cultural shifts, employees moving from one location to another, and related administrative tasks requiring experienced leadership oversight.

If you take the example of this healthcare merger further, imagine that in acquiring other companies you multiply the number of IT departments, medical records systems, and facilities that you have to keep track of almost overnight, or in just a couple short months. In this scenario, somebody's got to bring the various groups together, facilitate discussions to establish common goals, identify and work through resistance to change in the various departments, and ensure that the consolidation is executed as smoothly as possible.

And the complexity doesn't stop at the CEO's level. Chris Briggs, a chief of staff for Providence's chief information officer (CIO), reinforces the notion that many C-suite leaders in companies experiencing consolidation require more support to deliver initiatives and manage the staff. "It takes a special skill set to bridge what needs to happen at the staff and executive level in those circumstances," he says. If the C-suite executives were directly involved in all of the discussions that needed to take place, they would not be able to do anything else. Yet the CIO, for example, also has ongoing infrastructure issues to contend with, data integrity problems to solve, licensing renewals to negotiate with vendors, and compliance and policy issues with electronic record keeping to manage. These cannot be ignored. The chief of staff role enables the CIO to have more representation, and more direct representation, in more parts of the organization simultaneously.

In addition to a short- or long-term increase in complexity, your expansion into new lines of business—whether by acquisition, merger, or new product launch from within—can surface gaps in your current management team's skills and experience that might well be filled by a chief of staff. As documented in a study by Dan Marlin, Bruce Lamont, and Scott Geiger, the success of a company's diversification strategy depends on how well that strategy is matched to the strengths of its top management team members.[5] The success of a merger, for example, can depend not only on how integrated the joining firms become operationally, but also on how well suited the top executives are to manage the long-term change that is required. Further, different diversification strategies (concentric versus conglomerate) require different skills on the part of a company's top managers, and these factors should be taken into consideration before firms are joined. If your top executives are not well suited for at least a part of these new responsibilities, you can always find new leaders; but many CEOs found such black-and-white thinking too harsh and impractical. "Just hiring a new leader every time you encounter a gap can lead to a lot of babies being thrown out with bath water," said one CEO. "You lose a lot of good talent and vision that way."

A more nuanced approach is to use a chief of staff to fill the gaps while your leaders develop into more of the kind of leaders you want them to be. Examples from my research included chiefs of staff being hired to "bring emotional intelligence (EQ) to a high-intelligence-quotient (IQ) organization," to "put operational chops behind a visionary tech guru who doesn't have an organizational bone in his body," or to "smooth things over for a leader who comes across as gruff or doesn't play well with other people, while we work on that leader's people skills over time." Finally—and this last point needs to be stressed, too—in more cases than not, the chief of staff helps you manage your gaps. See "Leaders with Particular Styles, Strengths, and Positions" later in this chapter for more detail.

As companies grow, buy, and merge, you can see why so many chiefs of staff have titles like "Chief Integration Officer," "Sr. Director, Strategy & Ops, and Chief of Staff," "VP Planning and Operations," "Manager of Strategy and Planning," "Principal, Business Operations & Strategy." Even when it's not clear from their titles, many chiefs of staff describe their functions as something like "orchestrating the development and strategy for a business unit." They often come from growth and strategy functions, or go on to that kind of role from their chief of staff office.

## SPINOFF

Other organizations that use a chief of staff have recently been spun off of a larger company and are gaining their own foothold in the market without the former parent company. Spinoffs present their own leadership and management challenges. Even if you have only formal authority over the newly spun-off company, you still need resources and support from the originating organization until internal functions like HR, IT, and external areas like branding, customer base, and suppliers are in place. For a time, you might essentially be managing programs and constituents in two organizations while having formal control over only the (usually much more limited) resources of the new company. On the other hand, if you're the originating organization, in addition to your "day job," you've got some work to do to figure out what's going to be different without the group or groups that spun off. Does your structure still make sense? Do you need the same people, processes, and tools as you did before? A chief of staff role can be a great risk management tool on both sides of this coin.

When Royal Bank of Scotland (RBS) was directed to sell its insurance business, RBS Insurance, as part of a government intervention during the European financial crisis, Chief Executive Officer Paul Geddes had to form a new executive team in the midst of an extremely volatile transition, political backdrop, and marketplace.[6] This phased transition to Direct Line Insurance included a lot of financial and legal execution, exiting some team members for cost or other reasons,[7] and a massive IT infrastructure rebuilding.[8] Geddes brought a chief of staff into this situation, at first to translate the CEO's strategic intent to the new team and to broker the relationships between him and many of his new executive team members. He selected Chris Adams, who had previously served as chief of staff for Geddes. They worked well together because of complementary skills, and Adams helped organize the team's many activities. According to Adams, his work was primarily putting out fires at first—making sure the team knew what was expected of them, clarifying or working on execution where only high-level strategic guidance had been provided, and rooting out what wasn't working well. Over time, Adams's role became akin to a game of whack-a-mole, in which he'd take deeper dives into specific issues that arose, help the executive team troubleshoot and resolve problems, and ultimately put more standards in place so that the team could have more frequent access to Geddes and they could make the most of their time together.

When Advanced Micro Devices spun off its manufacturing arm (now GlobalFoundries), the CEO was going through a transition of the company's investor group in Abu Dhabi. The CEO needed someone with a cultural background in Middle Eastern affairs and Arabic language to manage all the moving parts in what was one important piece of a larger puzzle. So he hired Tareq Salaita, a project management specialist with a banking background, from within the company specifically to take some of the work from the CEO, to keep a finger on the pulse of the organization, and to advise the CEO on where he should be spending his time.

## BUSINESS DIVISIONS WITH THEIR OWN SUPPORT STRUCTURES, LIKE MARKETING, IT, AND FINANCE

If, instead of a more or less centralized, shared-services model, you have an organization with multiple divisions, each with its own support structures, a chief of staff can do the following:

- Help you mind the gaps in coverage between groups and ensure that duplicate work isn't a problem across groups.
- Identify and correct mismatches between tactical decisions made in various parts of the business (such as point-of-sale decisions or a key engineering process) and the broader organization's strategic goals.
- Ensure some level of governance and control where they are needed.
- Ultimately, perhaps multiple times during his or her tenure based on changing organization dynamics, assess and determine whether a shared-services model makes more sense and advising the executive on the best course of action.

Sometimes you will see work that needs doing that nobody is currently doing, or you will notice duplicate work being done in more than one organization. Your staff can help you spot these areas for improvement, but a chief of staff is in a unique position to help you not just see these gaps and overlaps but fact-check your assumptions about them (Are what appear to be gaps and overlaps actually what they appear to be? Are there reasons that alternatives haven't worked?) and then test various solutions with your staff and stakeholders until your team can bring you tangible, concrete solutions, alternatives, and recommendations. Your staff are busy driving their departmental goals, and a virtual team of representatives from one department or another to address a gap or an overlap might not share the sense of urgency, leading to a lag in addressing the problem and conflict or blame between groups. The chief of staff has the time to get deep on the issues, carries the weight of your office to make change a priority, and leads by influence and relational capital to get groups to share information or simply to make change happen and stick. He or she can facilitate discussions among, and enforce commitments between, the various divisions regarding roles and responsibilities so that people don't lose time and productivity arguing over whose job it is to do what. Finally, the chief of staff can get groups to share information, processes, or people who otherwise don't have an incentive to share.

In an organization in which one or more departments operate in a decentralized, somewhat independent fashion, decisions made at the local department level might not always align with broader organizational goals. One chief of staff I interviewed worked in an organization where each division operated independently, with its own set of money-making objectives, investors, and operating agreements. Some investors invested in all of the company's divisions, while some only invested in one division that most closely aligned to their interests. As a result, each division reported a different set of information to investors. Investors who invested in more than one part of the business complained that the reports from the various groups were inconsistent, hard to compare with each other, and in some instances raised more questions than they answered.

At the president's behest to clean up this situation, the chief of staff called for, planned, and—with the help of a trusted facilitator in HR—conducted an offsite with the various departments involved. They determined how they could better share and communicate similar information, even if each group still had its own reporting mandates for different investors. The conversations ranged from strategic decisions about what information to show investors to the formatting and presentation of the reports. Investors noted their satisfaction with the improvement in reporting after the next round of reports.

In one company's cost-reduction efforts, various parts of the business had seen headcount reductions, restructuring, and the implementation of new processes, while one division's engineering team—long seen as a core function and a sort of "sacred cow"—had grown over time and made only cosmetic changes to their processes. The chief of staff advised the president to consider championing bolder process changes and even moving to a model in which engineering itself was a shared service across several business units. Eventually, the president asked the chief of staff to help the teams involved plan for various scenarios, think boldly about new ways of doing things, and begin implementing changes based on those efforts.

The chief of staff can serve a number of governance functions. He or she can work across departments to set up governance frameworks through which information flows efficiently, the right people are tasked with reviews and approvals, people know their level of involvement (using RACI models or some similar method), and governance meetings are planned for and scheduled in advance. In one company that found itself in patent litigation, the chief of staff played a pivotal role in guiding decision making related to lawsuits. An increasing number of product groups in the company wanted the legal department, a shared-services group, to file patent infringement suits in court on their behalf. Each of these product teams brought requests to the legal department in a different format. The legal team were confident that they could build a solid legal case in many of these requests, but lawsuits are not cheap, and determining which suits to pursue, in which order, and which ones to say no to or revisit later, was a business decision, not legal one. These decisions required input from not only the product teams and the legal team but also the CFO, the corporate communications team, the president and executive leadership, and the board of directors. The chief of staff orchestrated discussions among the relevant stakeholders until the team finalized a litigation framework and governance process that enabled the company to proactively decide on its involvement in lawsuits instead of simply reacting to internal (or sometimes external) demands.

Even in medium-size companies with relatively simple reporting structures, you can find gaps and duplication—even more so in enterprise-level organizations with large divisions, each having their own core and support functions. Even where you implement lean transformation projects, the sheer volume of governance, people-management issues, data and reporting on ongoing operations, and cross-departmental projects can overwhelm you. The chief of staff serves to keep you out of the day-to-day management and details, and focused on the highest and best use of your time.

## GEOGRAPHICALLY DISPERSED TEAMS

About a third of the chiefs of staff I interviewed recounted traveling to overseas offices with their executives for product launches or to announce new leadership. Two of them found themselves in the midst of some pretty intense drama, one of them blocks away from a hotel bombing, the other in the middle of post-election riots, both having to coordinate security efforts and activate contingency plans for their executive's (or team's) safe exit in a highly chaotic and fluid situation. Although this scenario was not the norm for executives or their chiefs of staff, it is worth noting because of its relationship to the issue of geographic dispersion. Managing your agenda while in an environment away from familiar routines and resources can be challenging. These were extreme situations, of course. In most instances, the chief of staff's support was far more notable in the mundane activity of everyday management.

Specifically, if your organization spans more than two international locations or is separated by a day of time-zone differences (for example, Asia, North America, and Europe), a chief of staff can help do the following:

- Ensure that information and knowledge (not just the conclusions but at least some of the context) reach remote offices.
- Manage logistics of communicating across time zones, for ad hoc or infrequent meetings like an annual all-hands meeting or more regular gatherings like quarterly business reviews and executive leadership meetings.
- Involve remote workers in the co-located team from time to time, or consider when you need to travel to a remote site.
- Deal with culture clashes between offices.

Have you ever sent the action items from a big meeting to a remote team and expected them to run with it, only to find that the communication raised more questions for the team than it answered, resulting in a series of back-and-forth emails, phone calls, or video conferences to clarify and provide context? Knowledge transfer can be a problem in co-located teams, but it is a magnified and almost universal challenge with geographically dispersed teams (GDTs). A chief of staff can take this burden from you, in all but a few instances, by spending additional time with teams to provide translation of your strategic intent, to clarify details, and to hear concerns that can be fed back to you for further action.

Several executives in my interviews used a chief of staff to manage logistics of communication across time zones, especially when it came to meeting management. If you're having an ad hoc or infrequent meeting like an all-hands, with worldwide locations, the chief of staff can coordinate with all the vendors and internal teams to ensure the broadest reach of your meeting. He or she can advise you on—or decide—who attends the big meeting in person, who views it live by webcast or satellite broadcast, and who can watch the recording later. Correspondingly, he or she can ensure that remote participants have a way to submit questions during

Q&A sessions or after the meeting, and that the questions are read and summarized for your review and response at some point.

One of the universal challenges of remote or geographically dispersed teams is building trust between locations. The chief of staff is in a great position to help you spot disconnections between locations, whether headquarters and the remote locations or simply between remote locations. The chief of staff bridges these disconnections either through the involvement of remote team members with the co-located team or through your involvement with the remote teams. One executive was planning a semiannual leadership meeting designed to bring high-potential managers together with functional experts to solve intractable, cross-departmental challenges at the company. The chief of staff suggested that the meetings include at least one representative from the remote offices. The travel cost would be outweighed not only by their substantive contributions to the group but also by their feelings of inclusion and increased trust between team members who now had faces to put to names and a shared, in-person experience of working together. One executive at a U.S. headquarters kept receiving operating plans from an office in Beijing that were inconsistent with the (somewhat bold, ambitious) guidance she had given them. Her chief of staff sensed that a combination of cultural issues and so-called belief biases were causing the problem, and the best solution was for her to get on a plane and be present with the people to answer their questions. A visit by the president was seen as a sign of respect, and their ability to hear directly from her about her bold guidance helped them overcome their belief biases, resulting in a better plan in the next iteration. A trip to Beijing, while not cheap, was a small price to pay for better alignment and operating plans that worked.

## COMPETITIVE ADVANTAGE THROUGH TALENT DEVELOPMENT AND SUCCESSION PLANS

Having a chief of staff role—perhaps especially a rotational version of it—provides a unique leadership experience for high-potential talent in the company, creates bench depth in leadership at different levels, and helps you with formal succession planning for C-suite or staff-level positions. In other words, it's one tool for developing people into the kinds of leaders your company needs for long-term success. It can help you develop what David Ulrich and Norm Smallwood define as capabilities, or your organization's ability to reflect the strengths and competencies of its individual members.[9] The chief of staff can also help you more broadly identify and address talent and gaps throughout the organization because of his or her day-to-day exposure to people at all levels of the organization. Former Providence Health & Services CIO Laureen O'Brien says, "The largest cost driver in the healthcare IT budget is the cost of recruiting and retaining top IT talent; therefore the need for a strong chief of staff to help ensure the CIO is meeting the needs of the staff and working to continually develop and 're-recruit' top IT professionals." Most often, the chief of staff role is used to do the following:

- Take a high-potential employee, usually at a senior manager or director level, out of a specific functional role.
- Enable that person to see, learn about, and participate in the whole business and many, if not all, of its functions.
- "Re-enter" another function as a junior executive or general manager, based on business needs and the individual's career goals.

It's that re-entry point that gives you options. When one of your leaders moves within or out of the organization, for example, your chief of staff can be standing ready as a replacement, whereas just a short year or two ago that person would not have been ready to step into that vacant position. Given the chief of staff's particular strengths and development areas, you can also start to think about grooming that person to take on roles for particular leaders at some point in the future, probably not as his or her next job but a few years down the road.

While the role itself serves a development purpose, having the right person in the role can also help you more broadly identify and address talent gaps. The chief of staff, in the course of his or her daily duties, has closer and deeper access than you do to many of your future leaders and can get to know the relative merits of those leaders compared to the direction the organization is heading. The chief of staff can think about talent from a tactical point of view (Someone vacated an important role; is there an internal person to fill it?) or a capabilities point of view (We hired a bunch of task-oriented, technical people to start this company, but now we need people with EQ or people skills as we grow; or, We started as a bunch of creative types, and we need to pair them with someone with a process orientation if we're going to scale). In this way, the chief of staff can be a great advisor to you and your head of HR— or at least another point of view to counterbalance other points of view—as you manage human capital issues like talent development, succession planning, and restructuring.

The (especially rotational) chief of staff is also likely to be in the best position to identify or help you identify a list of potential successors for his or her own role. The current chief of staff knows as well as you where the role is heading and what skills, talents, and experiences are needed for the role as the company evolves around it. For a more detailed look at the opportunities and challenges of the rotational chief of staff role, see the section "Developing and Retaining Good People" in Chapter 3.

## INTERNAL ACTIVITIES, MEANT TO ADDRESS EXTERNAL COMPLEXITY, THAT END UP COMPOUNDING COMPLEXITY

I argued in Chapter 1 that the chief of staff role is, in part, a response to organizational complexity stemming from a number of mostly external factors. Many times, however, a company's internal activities that seek to address those complexities only compound them.[10] Further, leaders can be tempted to consider external complexity as the only kind and can fail to account for internal complexity, which is often evident in the day-to-day experiences of workers.[11] The chief of staff, having more regular access to people at all levels of the organization, can pick up on internal complexity before you do. He or she serves as an early warning system that indicates when something needs to be addressed, helps you conduct stakeholder analysis, helps you decide where each particular problem fits in the overall list of priorities, and brings potential solutions to the problem at the appropriate time. Whereas an activity might be designed to solve an element of external complexity, one benefit of having the chief of staff sitting in your office, overlooking all departmental-level activities, is that he or she can connect the dots between seemingly disparate activities and see the cumulative effect and unintended consequences of those activities in ways that people immersed in them might not. The early warning system works best when someone is reading the indicators from the workers and seeing what even they don't see.

## LEADERS WITH PARTICULAR STYLES, STRENGTHS, AND POSITIONS

The decision to use a chief of staff, and subsequent decisions about the emphasis or emphases needed in a chief of staff, is partly driven by the leader's leadership style, strengths and gaps, and his or her position relative to other organization and market dynamics. Given a recent Kapta Systems survey that found 45 percent of CEOs were not satisfied with their executive team's performance, the decision can also be driven by the leader's assessment of gaps in the leadership team.[12]

### The leader's style

With so much work to choose from on leadership styles (see the frameworks of Kurt Lewin; Robert Blake and Jane Mouton; Daniel Goleman, Richard Boyatzis, and Annie McKee; Eric Flamholtz and Yvonne Randle; and James McGregor Burns[13]) I could probably write a book focused on the chief of staff's utility relative to each of the leadership styles contained therein. However, my goal in this book is to keep this analysis at a fairly high level and to highlight some of the most common uses of the role from my interviews, as they relate to some of the most common leadership styles.

Some leaders with what I'd call bureaucratic tendencies (many times driven by high regulatory compliance and reporting requirements) might lean on a chief of staff primarily to manage governance processes, ensure that rules get followed, and ensure that risks are mitigated. In some cases, bureaucratic leaders in traditionally risk-averse companies, like insurance, found themselves needing to rethink outdated or traditional business models and sales channels, such as online customer portals and prepackaged services that added value to traditional product offerings. They hired a chief of staff with a strong background in change management, facilitation, and coaching to facilitate the executive and staff through the change process.

Several democratic, self-effacing, or servant leaders who highly valued collaboration leaned on their chiefs of staff to ensure that, among other things, they did not get politically blindsided or outmaneuvered by people in the organization with a more command-and-control, competitive style of leadership.

A few charismatic leaders, whose natural inclinations were more people-oriented and relational, looked to their chiefs of staff to fill the task-oriented needs on their team: to keep the executive informed; to fact-check materials (especially from the leader's "favorites," whom he or she would be inclined to take at face value); and to manage details, processes, and timelines.

I did not find a chief of staff working for any so-called autocratic or transactional leaders.

One thing in common among all the leaders who made the most of the chief of staff role was that they had no problem letting go of some direct control of day-to-day decisions and affairs, delegating to others, and taking the recommendations of their advisors. In fact, the executive's *unwillingness* to delegate was the number-one reason that HR executives said they saw the chief of staff role fail to be effective.

One long-time operating executive I talked to who consults with a number of technology companies in the Pacific Northwest told me about a potential client, a CEO for a tech company, whose business had quadrupled in just a couple years but who found himself embroiled in day-to-day operational challenges. He recognized that the best use of his time was promoting the product and helping potential customers see the vision of what his technology could do for their businesses. This leader named three to five specific areas where he should *not* be spending his time. The consultant explored with him the viability of a range of options, from hiring a chief operating officer or a chief of staff to hiring him (the consultant) on an interim basis until the potential client figured out what he would do long-term. In the end, the CEO agreed he needed help but just couldn't seem to pull the trigger on any of those options, and he remained entrenched in the day-to-day. In situations like these, boards of directors can heavily influence or direct CEOs to make the change they are hesitant to.

Without a chief of staff, David Cole oversaw the growth of a Weyerhaeuser subsidiary, Paragon Trade Brands, from $250 million to $700 million and 1,200 employees before taking the helm at Coinstar (now part of Outerwall). He oversaw Coinstar's growth from about $100 million to $917 million and from 500 to 1,500 employees. He credits his success to frequent customer visits; managing the internal workings of his organizations by walking around, visiting plants; asking questions on the shop floors based on data he received in executive leadership meetings; *and having a few key advisors in the organization,* including a couple financial analysts and a gifted executive assistant. He says, "I always had a few people I really trusted and leaned on, but I spoke to a range of folks to decide what reality was. In interviews with my EA candidates, I told them I was like Colonel Potter on *M\*A\*S\*H* looking for Radar O'Reilly—someone who can ask the questions before I do, handle my communications, and help me keep an ear to the ground." In his model of leadership, he did not choose to hire someone into a separate position like a chief of staff to manage day-to-day aspects of his role. But, he admitted, "There was a size of company—probably a couple thousand—where my hands-on style would max out and I'd have to consider a new range of options."

You are in the best position to know your leadership style. If you're not sure, a good coach should be able to walk you through an effective 360-degree review process and provide you with a pretty good picture. Then you can begin to consider more carefully how a chief of staff can complement your leadership.

## The leader's strengths

Your leadership style can arguably be viewed as a strength or a gap, but you have technical skills, soft skills, talents, and experiences that contribute to your performance as a leader. Your self-awareness of these areas is critical to understanding how a chief of staff might serve you and the organization.

One theme that emerged from my interviews was this notion of a chief of staff not just as someone who fills in the leader's gaps— what I'll call the complementarian model—but also as someone who can be so similar to the leader in strengths and background that he or she can project more of the leader in the organization. I call this the multiplicative model. Interestingly, although nearly every chief of staff and executive acknowledged the possibility of the multiplicative chief of staff, I could not find one. All of the 60-plus people I interviewed used or served in a complementarian model.

Some of my interviews turned up executives who were known as brilliant leaders in a field—software, law, branding—who by their own admissions didn't have an operational bone in their bodies and simply hired a chief of staff for operational support. Other leaders were operationally minded business generalists but needed someone with technical depth in their industry to bolster their general management street credibility or to help speak the language of their technical teams. In one $100 million company, the CFO was strong on financials (this should be obvious). He did not hire a chief of staff for financial brilliance but rather for orchestrating off-site meetings, driving team culture, and managing people. A chief of staff in one of Mexico's largest banks said, "I brought an outsider perspective, less technical than the team. I gave them another view. If I understand the leader's vision and ideas, the business will understand it. If I don't, they won't. My boss said, 'I don't need more tech people.'"

## The leader's position

First, you can start by considering your role in the organization and your primary stakeholders (see Figure 2.1). For a founder, president, or CEO, the primary stakeholders tend to be the board, investors, other industry leaders, customers, and your employees (not necessarily in that order—your focus is likely to shift based on the context and day of the week!). For a functional or divisional leader at the C-suite or VP (possibly senior director) levels, your primary stakeholders tend to be the founders, president, and CEO; the lines of business or your peers in the organization; and your own employees. These categories can overlap, of course. An example is if you are a CFO who is a functional or division leader but also very likely delivers earnings calls for investors, provides direct input to the board, and attends board meetings.

**FIGURE 2.1** Primary Stakeholders By Leadership Level*

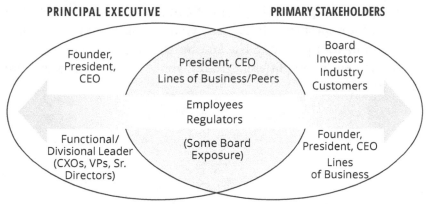

*Co-created with Colleen Hunter, Vivian Mason, and Slalom Consulting

For the founder, president, and CEO, you might have a heightened need for a chief of staff as your executive brand manager, with a sophisticated focus on and attention to PR and optics. As longtime Microsoft chief of staff David Pritchard says, "You might help your executive handle some complex PR requirements or issues like reporters calling you every few hours, knowing which ones to talk to and which ones to direct to the executive, and remembering that your words can shift the stock market." Farther down in the organization (especially in large companies), this kind of focus is not such a concern. Your formal position also influences the balance of forward-looking, strategic-thought partnership your chief of staff brings and his or her ability to oversee, execute, and deliver work that your staff are tasked with. Every chief of staff should be part thought partner, part executor; but the closer you go to the top of the organization, the more the blend skews toward the thinker.

In addition to your formal position in the hierarchy, what is your standing relative to the organization's current situation? Are you under tough financial pressures? If so, the nature and cause of those pressures can influence whether you hire a chief of staff and with what focus. Maybe you need someone with a sales operations background to drive change with the sales team, or someone with a distribution background to manage improvements or negotiate cost savings in the supply chain. Are you in a tight regulatory position? How well you're performing against compliance measures and the nature of any problems influences your decision. How long have you been in your position? The amount and type of help you need if you are new is very different than if you've been in the role more than six months.

## ◾ REFLECT & APPLY

After looking at the first pivot, organizational dynamics that lend themselves to a successful chief of staff role, I offer the following questions for assessment and reflection:

1. On a scale of 1–10, with 10 being the most complex, how would you rate the complexity of your leadership challenge? Why did you give it the rating you did?

   1     2     3     4     5     6     7     8     9     10

   _____

   _____

   _____

2. Of the organizational dynamics that tend to lend themselves to a successful version of the role, how many apply to your current organization or leadership situation?

| 1 | 2 |
|---|---|
| Medium to large size | Significant changes in leadership or organization structure |
| Multiple, diverse lines of business | Spinoffs |
| Business divisions with their own support structures | Internal activities end up compounding complexity |
| Geographically dispersed teams | |
| Competitive advantage through talent development and succession planning | |

   a. If you chose two or more of the dynamics in Column 1, you should work with your head of HR or an outside consultant to determine if you have a sufficient business case for the role in your organization.

   b. If you chose any of the dynamics in Column 2, begin the work in 2a.

   c. If you did not choose two or more dynamics from Column 1 or any from Column 2, your situation is not as likely to be a good fit for a chief of staff.

# 3

# Reported Benefits of the Chief of Staff Role

When the role is thoughtfully crafted and executed, a chief of staff can help you do many things, including the following:

- Focus on the highest and best use of your time.
- Execute or oversee work that has no clear departmental owner.
- Know what's really going on in your organization.
- Make and execute great decisions.
- Shorten your learning curve in a new company or industry.
- Ensure that the business functions when you are away.
- Develop and retain good people.

These benefits, which executives frequently report receiving from the role, form the basis of another pivot on which you can base your decision to hire a chief of staff.

## FOCUSING ON THE HIGHEST AND
## BEST USE OF YOUR TIME

"Above all, the CEO should focus on making the best forward-looking decisions about strategic direction. But to focus there means that other things can become inefficient. The chief of staff can facilitate the rest," says Tachi Yamada, chief medical and scientific officer at Takeda Pharmaceuticals.

To delegate so much sounds audacious. Risky. Like you're giving up the reins of power just when you should be feeling your most powerful. Yet history is littered with leaders who failed to get themselves out of the day-to-day affairs of a business and deal with long-term, strategic issues.[1] Harvard business professors Michael Porter, Jay Lorsch, and Nitin Nohria list as the number-one surprise for new CEOs: "You can't run the company."[2] They cite as the top two warning signs that you're struggling with this issue: "You are in too many meetings and involved in too many tactical discussions. There are too many days when you feel as though you have lost control over your time." As Lieutenant Rinaldi says in Ernest Hemingway's *A Farewell to Arms*, "I never think. No, by God, I don't think; I operate."[3]

In larger companies, this issue is about focusing on vision and strategy. In smaller companies where you will invariably remain in the weeds of sales or operations, it can be about just making sure that only the highest-priority items reach your desk.

To be fair, there are alternatives. You can just ignore everything on your desk that is not in your top three to five priorities. Some executives are incredibly disciplined and create disciplined cultures that enable this approach. Not every culture or leader exudes this kind of discipline, however. You can teach your people to handle, on their own, issues and projects that come from the bottom up, so that they don't reach your level. But the cross-departmental problems will almost always reach you in the end. You can pick one of your direct reports as your most trusted advisor, or lean on that person and a couple of respected thinkers and doers in the organization as your inner circle. Some executives I spoke with had successfully used this approach, but one of them in particular expressed the view that had the organization continued to grow in terms of employees or lines of business, this model would not have worked. Delegating to your executive team a number of special projects can spread your organization too thin (after all, having many priorities is the same as having no priorities). In addition, this approach can convey conflicting priorities: the sales people think they are working on the top-priority project that came from the top, and the product development people think the same thing, putting them at odds, while shared-services groups like HR and IT get caught in the middle of a resource turf war.

In many situations, you need someone in your organization with a reputation for getting things done; who can deal with as many issues as possible so that you don't have to; who doesn't have a particular departmental agenda; who has an analytical bent, can make sense of the unprecedented volume and sophistication of data you've got at your disposal, and translate it into options, proposals, and recommendations; and who can ensure that your strategic thinking is translated into action, measured, and adjusted over time. The chief of staff is perfect for this situation.

Former Providence Health & Services CIO Laureen O'Brien relied on Chris Briggs's project management professional (PMP) background in his chief of staff role, as he helped her manage the transition of seven regional information systems departments into one central function under O'Brien. O'Brien relied on Briggs to make rounds and help make sure folks were engaged. "While Laureen was looking forward and managing up," Briggs says, "I looked back and down to get people bought in, to handle the technical and operational things that helped her get where she wanted to go. I also bring the voice of the staff up to the executive level, listening to what's going on and making sure those concerns or feelings are known in the C-suite."

Tachi Yamada has seen the chief of staff role work well in multiple contexts, including the Bill and Melinda Gates Foundation and Takeda Pharmaceuticals. "The chief of staff can facilitate operations and special projects, following up on decisions that get made to ensure they're carried out and resolving issues that need resolving before they reach the executive." The more work that gets executed behind the scenes, the more time you have to focus on watching market, political, and people trends; thinking steps ahead of competitors; kicking off new products and services; thinking of ways to trim costs; being part of the company's public face and meeting with strategic partners; or otherwise keeping investors happy.

### Funnel, filter, facilitator

The chief of staff is not just about you having someone to whom you can give unidirectional orders to get stuff done. It is as much about having a trusted partner who can funnel, filter, or facilitate work on your behalf, freeing you to focus on the highest and best use of your time. The chief of staff identifies issues that can be done, delegated, or deferred so that you see or worry about only the ones that you need to. There are some issues the chief of staff might not even mention to you, some that he or she might not mention until they are already resolved, and others for which the chief of staff might give you a heads-up that there is an issue and that it's being dealt with. This person might even advise you that now is not the time for you to get involved with the issue or issues on the table. Then the chief of staff would use his or her sense of all that is going on in the organization to keep you grounded in the big picture.

What I originally thought of as a gatekeeper role turned out to be something more nuanced as my interviews unfolded. One chief of staff used the analogy of the chief of staff as a distiller or funnel versus a filter, and what he meant is that the chief of staff shouldn't limit the flow of information between the "shop" and the executive but rather sift, analyze, prioritize, and make the flow as efficient as possible. In his situation, that worked. Some executives, though, wanted a filter. They wanted many fewer items coming across their desk because they spent way too much time in the details of problems that others should have been solving. Others described the chief of staff as someone who took care of certain items, yes, but also prioritized, brokered, and facilitated certain meetings between the executive and others in the organization, especially if the topics were likely to generate heated debate or involved individuals whose voices might otherwise not be heard. "As a facilitator, I clarified statements made by my boss after meetings, unblocked issues, got time on the executive's calendar for those who needed it most, provided more visibility to my VP for teams abroad, and dealt with some people who had issues that they were hesitant to go directly to my VP with."

In my view, the information funnel, filter, facilitator role is among the most important of a chief of staff's varied roles. If he or she prioritizes the wrong kinds of issues, the chief of staff, and perhaps the role itself, will be seen as a wedge between an executive and the organization, a status symbol for the executive's inflated sense of ego, and an unnecessary layer of bureaucracy. However, a well-crafted filter, combined with an efficient funnel, combined with a facilitator for everything that's left, can keep you from becoming insulated, can help you dig deeply on only the issues that you need to address, and can also help you focus on your more forward-looking, strategic responsibilities instead of having to dip into the details of the operations on a frequent basis. Some executives want a filter, some want a funnel, and all want a facilitator.

## Willingness to delegate and the importance of trust

One thing to keep in mind about the highest and best use of your time is your own willingness to delegate. The best chief of staff in the world won't help you if you are not willing to cede control of some of the details. The executive's unwillingness to delegate was the number-one reason that the role failed, according to HR executives I interviewed. When this topic came up in multiple interviews, I dug further. I asked why executives didn't trust someone else to do some of the day-to-day activity that bogs them down, and who owns that burden of trust? Was the executive simply unwilling to let go, or had the chief of staff stumbled early in some way or diminished the trust? There were two answers. One, nearly all chiefs of staff will have a "stumbling moment" early in their tenure. Taking on a lot of responsibilities that they are not already familiar with is often part of their development in the role. Part of your leadership as the executive is in how you give the chief of staff space to fail, learn, and move on. Also, in the majority of times, the senior executive had the best of intentions but simply wasn't comfortable giving up control. For more information about trust and giving the chief of staff room to make a few mistakes, see Chapter 6, "What Should I Expect in the First 90–100 Days?" More than half the executives I spoke with stressed that because of the amount and types of work you might be placing on the chief of staff's shoulders, you had better be sure that you trust that person and that, in your hiring process, you look for what some called "the X factor"—not just the skills but some kind of connection or trust on a personal level—in the first interview.

## EXECUTING OR OVERSEEING WORK THAT HAS NO CLEAR DEPARTMENTAL OWNER

You almost always have projects that span multiple departments. Some executives handle this kind of work by assigning it to the department that is the closest match. Others rotate special projects across their leadership team. This week, the head of communications gets to drive it, next week the CIO, and so forth, until all leaders have driven a special project and the rotation begins anew. Still others will split the project among two cosponsors. These are not always good options. Your people are focused on their departmental/functional point of view, and that's good. You want your sales folks focused on sales, for example, and not peripheral tasks. You might encourage creative competition among groups, but unless you've got the dream team of leaders, you might find each of your executive staff at various stages between fully engaged and burned out, following their own career ambitions, and steeped in their own silos or histories (productive or not) with other departments. These factors can make it tricky to pick the right, least biased owner.

Project ownership can be particularly murky for new or disruptive projects that also happen to be cross-departmental. Unless heavy incentives are attached, an executive sponsor on your team who is "voluntold" to drive a project is far less likely to give it the attention it needs, especially when that sponsor compares the project against his or her already-in-progress, high-priority goals. Splitting the project among multiple owners can be problematic, too. As the saying goes, if there are multiple owners, there is no owner. Work without an owner is unlikely to get done.

For the chief of staff, part of managing cross-departmental work is simply clarifying ownership after work is assigned, usually in a staff meeting of some kind. Melanie Willis's service as chief of staff for multiple executives involved in a commercial airliner's final assembly, which I mentioned earlier, came during a historic period of tension between management and labor. She would stay behind after meetings and engage with folks, asking, "Did you all get what you needed? Did you have any questions?" And, after that discussion, it was important to close with what the executive expected to see from each team or individual team members next time, which left little ambiguity as to who owned what. In the rare event that an item remained unresolved, she would bring it back to the executive and follow up with the teams as needed. I'll cover this follow-up and project management role in more detail in the section on "Making and Executing Great Decisions" later in this chapter.

Sometimes, though, the work has much bigger implications. When a Fortune 100 software company decided to defund one senior executive's R&D darling project and roll the software from that project into the company's flagship software, the senior executive whose project was defunded leaned on his chief of staff more than at any other time in their work together. The situation was emotional because everyone wanted to be a part of a product that overcame the heroic journey to marketplace success, and after years of hard work there had been signs of that success. The executive and his chief of staff had to get the leadership team together and focused on how to find an alternative solution to the product they'd been working on and not waste the investment the company had already made in the product. Their emotional state and departmental objectives made it clear that they couldn't drive this work on their own. The executive essentially told the leadership team, "You won't all be involved in defining the next step for this business. My

precisely because of her ability to stand above the line or core functions. His business is one of science. If Mancuso were a line or core leader, she would likely come with a bias toward a particular line of scientific inquiry or theory at the expense of others; but as a business generalist she is thinking more broadly about distribution and sales channels, what the market will bear, legal and compliance issues, PR, or people management issues that can all affect the outcomes of special projects.

## KNOWING WHAT'S REALLY GOING ON IN YOUR ORGANIZATION

Without a chief of staff, you risk experiencing the negative effects of one of the core truths of executive leadership: It's lonely at the top.[6] You will rarely receive direct, constructive criticism or positive feedback from above or below you—about your performance, about specific decisions that you made, or about your strategic direction. Plus, information from the lower levels of the organization tends to get filtered through several layers of management on its way to you. That information is frequently so sanitized by the time it reaches you that it omits pertinent details or trade-offs that would make for better decisions on your part. The result is negative surprises.

In a recent survey of 300 chief executives, Chris Wells of Kapta Systems found that "38% of CEOs were blind-sided by a negative surprise in the past 90 days."[7] According to Michael Porter, Jay Lorsch, and Nitin Nohria, the number-three surprise for new CEOs is that it is hard to know what is really going on.[8] Granted, you can't know everything. But as you climb, the consequences for not knowing are more significant, and the tolerance by boards, founders, and even courts or juries might be lower. In Chapter 1, I discussed policy and regulation and how, as an officer of the company, you might have fail-and-go-to-jail responsibilities for certain aspects of your business. And we all know how well the "we didn't know" defense worked out for Jeffrey Skilling and his cohort of Enron executives.[9]

Still, not every crisis ends up with someone in jail. You might simply think everything is moving along just fine when revenue falls short for the quarter or costs suddenly jump. Or you go into a board meeting thinking your key leaders are aligned and moving forward, when all of a sudden you find out they're all over the map, and each of you loses face with the board. In many levels of an organization, you can solve your isolation problem through having more, or more focused, information channels, but the higher up the ladder you go, the more filtered the information becomes. You have to challenge it constantly. It's the chief of staff's job to know which doors to knock on so that you get what you need and avoid negative outcomes.

One chief of staff recalled two instances in which a cross-department team had been assigned a joint recommendation to the board, only for the chief of staff to discover a day or two before the board meeting that the teams had not even met to discuss a proposal. In each case, a (different) designated project leader was telling the president that the teams were on track to deliver the recommendations. Only as the chief of staff finalized the agenda and content for the meeting, and was preparing his boss to think about talking points on the agenda items, did he discover this disconnect. A product team leader had one point of view, the head of sales had another, and the general counsel a third, and the points of view required reconciliation. It was okay—even expected—that people would have different points of view. It was not okay for the different points of view to not be known by all the team members, discussed, and presented in a constructive way to the board. Walking into the board meeting this way in the past had made the entire leadership team look disorganized and fragmented.

The board had reacted previously to this kind of disarray with irritation and frustration. Meaningful decisions became lost in the ensuing debate, fist-pounding, and shouting. A decision that happened to be clear unintentionally benefited one department at the expense of others, leading to most departments resisting the implementation of the decision. Then, six months later, everyone wondered why the decision had yielded few to none of the intended outcomes. The staff were pointing fingers and enmeshed in blame games. The credibility of the entire leadership team, including the president, had been undermined. In the current situation, if not for the chief of staff's relationships and walk-around in preparing the boss for the big meeting, this disconnect would have gone undetected until they "walked into the chipper shredder." The team ended up working on a Sunday afternoon before a Monday board meeting to discuss some key points of disagreement and to frame some options for the board. Sunday meetings did not win the president any popularity contests, but the whole chain of events established that the chief of staff was not looking out for his own interest, or even just the president's, but their collective interest and reputation.

One former chief of staff at a major U.S. professional services firm said part of her role was that of the fair witness from Robert Heinlein's novel *Stranger in a Strange Land*, an individual who is trained to see the world very literally and not infer anything beyond what is readily observable.[10] Her approach was not making too many assumptions, regularly checking the assumptions she did make, and not speaking falsely if she wasn't sure. Using this approach, she was able to notice and advise her executive on trends in operations, systems, and technology as their office moved from decentralized, local control to more control by the national office. Further, she was better able to guide the broader team through these changes.

The advantage of leaning on a chief of staff for these functions is that the breadth and depth of his or her relationship with you and other leaders throughout the organization provide him or her—and by extension, you—with a cross-departmental viewpoint that few others have. The chief of staff can also use discretion in handling confidential information to bring to light the insights that you might not see in your scorecard numbers. But this individual can do this only if time has been spent on something I mentioned earlier—what one chief of staff called "sneaker diplomacy," the management by walking around that you might crave and occasionally do but never have enough time for. It's at the core of the chief of staff's job.

Maybe your crisis is that one of your superstar staff members—one of your favorites—is meeting or exceeding his or her target results numerically but leaving a trail of broken relationships, burned-out people, or other misery along the way because everyone is afraid to tell you how the star behaved. A chief operating officer I interviewed recounted just such a time:

> I had transferred from one business unit to another and brought along an HR person with me. That person stayed with me for about a year and then left. Only then did I start hearing that the person I had brought with me was widely regarded as a jerk. As I solicited more stories about this person, I realized I had brought along with me someone who was behaving like a jerk, and nobody told me. I was so disappointed that nobody felt they could say it. It's important to have people around you who feel free to say, "You know, I know you like that person (or issue), but there's a problem...." Then I can decide the appropriate course of action for that person or issue.

Gaining an accurate picture of what is really going on in your organization, beneath all the filters that people put on the information to "help" you digest it, is an effort worthy of heroic mythology. Many obstacles stand in your way. First, your leaders and staff might not always be transparent about or even aware of their own agendas, career aspirations, and goals. Second, it's not easy for your executive team to speak truth to your power. Regardless of your assurances that there won't be retribution for unpopular opinions, most people have experienced retaliation of some sort in their past, and it takes a tremendous amount of courage for your subordinates to move beyond the defense mechanism that comes from those experiences and bring the truth to you. It takes trust, and trust takes time, which you don't often have a lot of. Finally, all of these issues take time and effort to get to the bottom of, while you're addressing operational issues, managing fire drills, being the public face of the company, and, oh, by the way, trying to focus on the strategic, visionary portion of your job that you were really hired for.

To avoid the problem of isolation, you need someone who can do these things:

- Monitor the periphery of activity in your team, looking for warning signs and investigating when necessary.
- Invest more time than you can walking the halls, where he or she can get the input, feel, and mood of employees in different corners of the office; in other words, someone who can "read the tea leaves" in the organization accurately.
- Serve as an information filter, previewing information and applying critical analysis and coaching to the teams under you so that before you see information, it's been fact-checked and validated.

The flip side of your not knowing what's going on in the organization is that many folks in the organization don't know what's going on in the C-suite. The same Kapta Systems study that I cited earlier found that only 22 percent of CEOs have confidence that their employees "get it" relative to the company's strategy. Sometimes, no matter how many times you communicate a message—in a memo to employees, at a town hall or all-hands meeting, or by walking the halls yourself—people just don't fully get the implications until someone explains it to them. A chief of staff can direct and clarify communication from the top down and the bottom up, which can enable the entire organization to be better aligned. The chief of staff can also, as part of his or her investment of time spent walking the halls, reinforce key messages from the top that might or might not have sunk in at the lower levels.

## MAKING AND EXECUTING GREAT DECISIONS

Most of the easy decisions in the organization have already been made by the time something lands on your desk. The remaining decisions are the kinds that might not have clear—or even good—answers but require deep understanding of multiple possible

## UNIVERSAL COMPETENCIES

### Servant leadership or managed ego

I describe servant leadership/managed ego to some extent in "Universal Competencies" in Chapter 5. Additional insights from my interviews include these:

- A chief of staff must represent you but *is not* you. He or she must never confuse these.
- A chief of staff should be "steely"—that is, grounded in the company's values, goals, and your (the executive's) direction. The chief of staff is not easily rattled when things don't go as expected and, indeed, might operate best in crises.
- A chief of staff doesn't always feel compelled to contribute in meetings but is always attuned to what's going on in case called upon.
- A chief of staff must be able to learn from everybody in the organization, from entry-level employees to the board of directors.
- A chief of staff walks a line between carrying out your directives, which might not be popular with staff, and listening to and serving the staff's needs as well.

One chief of staff says this: "You need to be able to walk into the offices of people who outrank you and are compensated very differently than you and tell them hard truths or ask them for significant favors, and you have to understand that even though your merit landed you in your position and gave you access to your boss, your access is not sufficient by itself to make those demands or requests. That's a very difficult line to walk and still have people like you."

Amanda Mancuso at SCYNEXIS says, "You don't succeed in the role looking out for number one—you succeed by looking out for and balancing the needs of multiple stakeholders. There's a difference between servant leadership and servitude. You don't have to be a doormat to meet needs."

scenarios and the relative risks and trade-offs in each of those scenarios. What's worse, if your executive leadership team are working well together or exceeding expectations, you might actually be in more danger than ever of making bad decisions. This risk is present because the more cohesive your team, the more likely they are to make decisions based on the knowledge they already have and to discount knowledge that is not as well known, regardless of how true it might be.[11] Such cohesion can contribute to groupthink, which brought us such famous business disasters as the Deepwater Horizon oil spill, the financial collapses of 2008 (in the United States) and 2011 (in Europe), the grounding of Swissair, and the major setbacks at Marks & Spencer and British Airways between 1998 and 2001.[12]

Cohesion can also make it easier for yes-people to overcommit without fully thinking through their position on an issue. You and your staff might be open and honest with each other and think that people are free to say what they want and not be yes-people. At some point, though, it's not appropriate for you to voice every concern, doubt, or frustration you think or feel in front of the group, and your team might not want to be seen as hesitating or saying no. In those moments, they will commit to actions they really don't agree with, which can lead to their resistance in carrying out even clear decisions. Sometimes a decision might have been clear to you but not so clear to the team. Somebody has to "bird-dog" the multiple decisions, strategic initiatives, and special projects in your organization, help the staff prioritize, and ensure that decisions are carried out in accordance with your original intent.

To help you make and execute great decisions, the chief of staff serves as analyst and decision framer on the one hand and project manager, change agent, and coach on the other.

## Analyzing and framing decisions

Leon Panetta, who served as the second chief of staff to U.S. President Bill Clinton, says this of the government chief of staff position: "A very important role for a chief of staff is to—in a very concise way, because of the number of decisions the president has to make—to tee those decisions up and make sure the staff gives him the options on which to decide."[13] This is one area where the business chief of staff can borrow from government.

As in government, a corporate chief of staff helps you explore a broader range of possible scenarios, risks, and trade-offs than you or your leadership team otherwise would, so that you can arrive at better decisions. The chief of staff digests and summarizes reams of quantitative and qualitative data related to markets, projects, programs, and budgets in nearly every corner of the business. He or she fact-checks far more data than you can on your own and requests that additional reporting be made available, if necessary. As your thought partner, the chief of staff helps you consider the voices of people who are not in the room when decisions are being made; the political realities of where you stand today compared with your support bases inside and outside the company; who can be persuaded toward a particular point of view; and which battles are worth fighting. Only then does your chief of staff frame for you the possible scenarios and options, the relative risks and trade-offs of each, and recommendations for your ultimate decision.

One potential roadblock to making and executing good decisions is your shadow side or your staff's shadow side. In an interview with McKinsey's Olivier Sibony and Allen Webb, Randy Komisar of Kleiner Perkins Caufield & Byers shares the insight that rather than pretending we don't have biases, we should actively acknowledge and manage our biases.[14] We all think or behave in ways that do not appear to others as fully rational, having allowed our blind spots or shadows to get the better of us in the moment. In fact, there's mounting evidence in brain science that none of us make decisions as rationally as we think we do.[15] The chief of staff can reflect to you reality that you don't see.

If you're in a meeting trying to decide whether to pursue sales in a new market, for example, everyone in the room has an explicit agenda. You might be asking, "How am I going to justify this to the board or investors?" The departmental or functional leaders are asking, "How are we going to carry this out and how will it land with employees?" Everyone has hidden agendas, too. For example, very few of your staff are going to say, "Well, I was hoping the company was going to pursue another path that is in my area of expertise, and I was hoping to position myself as senior VP when that happened." And you are not likely to tell everyone at a meeting that you are scared to death that if this path isn't successful, you're out of a job.

"The chief of staff doesn't have to play the game," says one high-tech chief of staff, "but you have to know a game is being played. Within that, you have to know what people want from your boss (or you) and then decide what you're going to do." Because of his or her breadth and depth of relationships, the chief of staff can bridge all these agendas and sources of resistance, surface them at the appropriate times, and ensure that they are dealt with thoughtfully and with solutions that have formed only after as many variables as possible in the time frame are known.

Sometimes the lack of clarity about decisions or who owns what can result from poor meeting management. You might be as susceptible as others to thinking out loud in meetings or getting caught in the details of an issue instead of focusing on the big picture. You might care about the decision made and be eager to assign an owner, but you are usually not going to be focused on tracking all the decisions in a meeting, who was assigned what for each one, and knowing who to follow up with, when. Several C-suite executives recounted for me stories about occasions when they contributed ideas in brainstorming sessions with their staff that never got acted on, probably because they were perceived to be casual ideas, parking lot items, or weren't called out specifically as action items with clear owners. If the tasks weren't spoken explicitly or emphatically, or nobody was assigned the work, then nobody took responsibility and did the work. Then, one day an animated founder, investor, or board member pounded his fist on the desk, wondering why nobody had addressed this issue when he'd been raising it for a long time (in one case that came up in my interviews, three years!). A chief of staff can be a great option for handling these kinds of things:

- Keeping the meeting moving from one agenda item to the next in a timely fashion, with your agenda in mind.
- Gaining any needed clarification about actions, assignments, or strategic intent while others are focused on expressing their departmental viewpoints or discussing other details.
- Keeping track of all the decisions, action items, owners, and time lines agreed to in meetings for later follow-up.

- Clarifying the urgency or relative priority of action items, in situations in which the staff might not want to be seen by the boss as hesitating or saying no.

The chief of staff plays a role in helping you manage the rhythms of your business—especially the cadence of regular leadership and governance meetings—but the chief of staff can also be your main meeting manager. Of course, your executive assistant can provide a certain amount of support in scheduling the meeting, ensuring the right attendees are present, getting audiovisual or call-in information to remote participants, and ensuring content is delivered on time for review and discussion. But for long meetings, most executive assistants I spoke to also have to manage the arrival and departure of snacks and lunches and field inquiries to the executive's office while the executive is in the meeting, which typically keeps the EA out of the meeting. Because of the chief of staff's role in shaping the agenda with you (having business context for the discussion) and being your shadow, he or she can be your main point of coordination inside and during the meeting. He or she can manage who's calling in by phone and who's attending by video, make sure that participants are only on the phone for the discussions they are privy to and that everyone else is off the line or out of the room, and communicate with team members as to whether their segment of the meeting is running on time, ahead of schedule, or behind. He or she might even have the IT department on speed dial during critical times to ensure minimal disruption to the meeting due to technical issues. Many executives leaned on their chiefs of staff to give them time checks when they were engrossed in the conversation and to pass notes with observations about the dynamics between people in the room.

All of these roles and benefits help you to manage your leadership and leadership team's brand inside and outside the organization while ensuring that you are making and preparing to execute better decisions.

# UNIVERSAL COMPETENCIES

### Political savvy

I describe political savvy to some extent in the section "Universal Competencies" in Chapter 5. Additional insights from my interviews include these:

- A chief of staff must be your (the executive's) eyes and ears to what's going on in the organization, because not knowing can be devastating. He or she collects information by dealing in a depth of relational currency that you can't get on your own: more time walking the halls, meeting over coffee with your staff, understanding people's agendas and the complexities they face in their jobs more fully.

- A chief of staff needs to demonstrate ethical behavior, including tact, discretion, and know-how to safeguard or use confidential information.

- A chief of staff must understand formal and informal power and manage your brand.

On relational currency, one chief of staff says, "About 85 to 90 percent of the time, I'm not demanding something of anyone. I'm working with them. I've got my sleeves rolled up with them. Or I'm listening to someone when she pops her head in, or I'm walking the halls. Making that time for those relationships is invaluable, especially for the 10 percent of the time that I have to demand something."

One company president says, "My chief of staff's first challenge was managing a person who'd been passed over for the chief of staff role. Talk about trial by fire! He sometimes knew about people being managed out or managed up in the organization, and he had to gather information tactfully, make decisions, and act while safeguarding that knowledge." For some people, handling confidential information is black and white— you don't share it. Sometimes that's true, but a chief of staff knows how to share even confidential information in a way that can be useful to the organization, either in pieces but not in whole, or in the aggregate and at a high enough level that it points people in the right direction without giving away crucial details.

A high-tech chief of staff says of power and brand management, "Sometimes the leader thinks something is important while the rest of the organization doesn't. If the executive continues to push it, he or she can lose credibility. The chief of staff has to advise the executive on which battles to fight."

## Managing projects and change, and coaching

Your departmental/functional leaders can and should also support decision making through analysis and decision framing. The advantage of a chief of staff is that he or she can focus across departments, track decisions through to completion, and coach you and the team through decision making as well as change and resistance.

The first order of business for executing decisions is clarifying what work needs to be done, by whom, and in what order, and putting a stop to work that is not meant to be done. This begins with clarifying strategic intent. Amanda Mancuso didn't set out to be a corporate chief of staff, but Yves Ribeill, CEO at SCYNEXIS, noticed that people followed her to her office after meetings because they wanted her interpretation of what was said in those meetings: "Did I hear this right? When Yves said X, did he mean X, or did he really mean Y or Z? Is this consistent with other projects and initiatives in the organization?" They followed Mancuso because she had a knack for correct interpretation and guiding leaders and teams to generally positive outcomes based on her answers to these questions. Mancuso noticed what was said and not said in a meeting in a way that was not always obvious to the staff or was not always raised in a way that was useful to them. She helped them act on Yves's strategic intent. The more this happened, the more the staff trusted Mancuso, the more she stayed connected to what was going on in the organization, and the more she was able to ensure that the right work was being done by the right people at the right time. A president in a high-tech firm went so far as to tell me that if people didn't come to her chief of staff for translation, she was not being disruptive enough. Michelle Fleury, who served in two chief of staff roles at Cisco, adds, "Other people than your leader have influence on the outcome. If you're not aware of them and managing them, you won't get great decisions or support. Sometimes you have decisions that get made and reversed. The decision-making event is like negotiating overseas; it can be a point in time. If you want results, not just decisions, you have to manage it."

Clarifying strategic intent also means identifying work that should *not* be done. Numerous executives told me about what they

# UNIVERSAL COMPETENCIES

### Translation and interpretation

I describe the translation and interpretation competency in the section on "Universal Competencies" in Chapter 5. Additional insights from my interviews include these:

- A chief of staff needs to be keenly in tune to the team dynamics and agendas of various stakeholders and help you manage those and ensure the delivery of your strategic intent.

- A chief of staff must be able to "read" you and the organization for your potential reactions to differing courses of action.

One chief of staff says, "It's hard to quantify the ability to 'read a room' or translate what was said in a meeting into action. This doesn't sit well with people in a data-driven culture, but clearly some people have a knack for taking more effective action than others after walking out of the same meeting as others. The chief of staff has an intuition based on past experience and has to know how to use it."

thought of as a casual comment in a meeting that resulted in teams of people scrambling to achieve something that might or might not have been a real business priority. After his company signed a licensing deal with a company that produced televisions, one CEO said to his leadership team that he sure would love one of those TVs, with his company's brand, in his office someday. This resulted in a division head diverting (in this situation, wasting) precious resources on creating a TV in his company's own lab, whereas the CEO had only wanted someone to buy him one of the existing TVs. Another executive I spoke to made what he thought was a casual comment to some direct reports about not being crazy about the color of the walls in his office suite. When he came to work the following Monday morning, the walls had been repainted. He admitted he liked the new paint, but he cringed to think that some poor painter had worked all weekend on this job and one of his own departments had spent the money on it, when he had never intended for anyone to actually repaint his office. It's easy for staff to lose the context without someone asking the right questions, spotting superfluous activity or disconnects, and being the person the team could go back to for clarity without feeling like they're challenging the boss.

The chief of staff is someone with whom you can explore "what if" scenarios that you don't want to distract or worry your departmental/functional leaders with (yet). He or she isn't only concerned with the substance of decisions you have to make but will pay particular attention to, and partner with you on, the *way you have conversations* with your staff, board members, and investors, and the ways they have conversations with each other. He or she can be your first sounding board on your approach to the conversation you want to have, one who knows that much of what's said will fall to the cutting room floor. Finally, he or she can help you think about your priorities and which battles you want to fight. Cisco's Fleury adds, "The chief of staff asks, 'Is there more happening than we can get done?' and 'Are we trying to do too much?' It's about helping the executive stay focused on the priorities or let something go. You need this sounding board to clarify your thinking, and your chief of staff, having been there with you through that process, can help clarify your intent later on in the most appropriate ways.

As I noted in the section on "Analyzing and Framing Decisions," a chief of staff as coach can question your ideas before they are committed to action and reflect realities that you and your team might not see. The realities that you haven't yet seen might be the dissenting viewpoints but might also be information that the team was not yet aware of. In this way, the chief of staff can help prevent groupthink and cause the yes-people in the room to more fully consider their position before committing to action.

"The $50 Million Question" story that I started this book with is a great example of the chief of staff in this coach role. In that story, the chief of staff made dissent safe by focusing on and verifying what the group wanted and asking questions around that, even if it felt like publicly questioning the boss. This ability is critical for a chief of staff. Maybe others in the room felt as he did but also felt the pressure to make revenue numbers and didn't want to be the ones seen as saying no to more money unless there was a strong legal or moral reason to do so.

Often, in the meeting at which a big decision needs to be made, you've got your point of view, and you might even be ready to decide and give orders to execute in a particular way. Maybe your chief of staff or one or more members of your leadership team has already done a certain amount of brainstorming and challenging with you about this topic. Let's say your chief of staff has also had closed-door conversations with a VP who is not bringing forth her full perspective in the big meeting, who doesn't want to be seen as publicly disagreeing with the boss or not being a team player. Or maybe the executives on your team aren't sure if now's the time to raise the objection with you or if the ship has sailed. You can coach your leaders on a lot of these issues. You can create a robust culture of debate, per Liz Wiseman and others.[16] You can make assurances that there won't be retaliation. You can make it safe.

Yet these actions require high degrees of trust, time, and culture change that you might not have, and the assurance that you won't retaliate against dissenting views is often read by members in the room as a secret code for its opposite. The chief of staff has the least to lose by raising controversial points of view on behalf of team members who *do* have a lot to lose. Sometimes, though, the chief of staff's role is to help the team say what needs to be said themselves, and to have the courageous conversations they need to have, by raising the issue in such a way that everyone is open to hearing it.

I've referred before to Melanie Willis, who served as chief of staff during some historic labor negotiations related to the assembly of a commercial airliner. She says, "The idea was being a safe space for both sides by being real and open and by over-communicating. People might not bring something up with the boss during a meeting or even after it, but if you can sense it based on your previous conversations with them and put it out there, the issue gets addressed in a way that nobody feels threatened." This position at the table enables the chief of staff to be more than a PowerPoint driver, a reporting jockey, or a behind-the-scenes budget zombie.

In the meeting, the chief of staff watches who's dominating the conversation, who hasn't spoken, who's getting agitated, or who's

# UNIVERSAL COMPETENCIES

## Coaching

I describe the coaching competency, as it relates to the chief of staff, in "Universal Competencies" in Chapter 5. Additional insights from my interviews indicate that the chief of staff must be able to do the following:

- Actively listen (at least half of respondents called this out as *the* most critical skill). Listening underpins the chief of staff's ability to gather information, uncover and understand hidden agendas, broker relationships, and develop workable solutions.
- Question your ideas before they are committed to action.
- Expand your thinking by reflecting the reality that you or your staff might not see, in a way that you might be open to it.

One chief of staff says, "Listening is about hearing multiple versions of the same story and understanding how they can all be right from the perspective of the people involved (with no malice; people just understand things differently) and also putting it all together to get a full picture."

A CEO told me, "A coach has a learning orientation and curiosity that is important to understanding the points of view of my staff and key people in the organization, helping me make better decisions, and helping me get the right work done more quickly. That learning orientation can keep us all from being as controlled by our biases as we otherwise would be."

One real benefit of the chief of staff as trusted advisor and thought partner is having someone, in a low-risk environment for you, with whom you (or your staff) can be completely honest, express your deepest concerns and uncertainties, and even vent, whether or not those expressions are appropriate for public forums or subsequent conversations. These interactions enable the chief of staff to speak truth to your power (a courageous act) or raise contrarian points of view in a nonconfrontational way. Leon Panetta says of his days in the White House, "Somebody's got to be the go-to guy on difficult issues, who can go into the Oval Office and deliver a very tough message to the president. You can't do that if you got eight or nine guys sitting around saying, 'Well, you go tell him.' 'No, it's not my turn to tell him, you tell him.'"[17]

shutting down as the conversation progresses. Outside of meetings, he or she notices who's meeting with whom, and who is not meeting even if they should be meeting. As dot-connector, the chief of staff uses his or her tribal knowledge of how things actually get done, combined with broad and deep relationships, to connect efforts in one part of the business with efforts in another. Both

## ENSURING THAT THE BUSINESS FUNCTIONS WHEN YOU ARE AWAY

At the top levels of leadership, you often have duties that take you away from headquarters: investor meetings, visits to manufacturing facilities or remote locations, business development and customer-focused meetings, natural and man-made disasters that put business continuity at risk, conferences and training, service on boards and nonprofits, speaking engagements that support your leadership platform and contribute to your leadership brand, and vacations. A chief of staff is invaluable for these types of situations, either for triaging and routing requests to the appropriate parties for decisions or serving as your proxy when appropriate.

The chief of staff works with you and your executive assistant to do the following:

- Determine, months in advance, a travel calendar that minimizes your travel around critical times in the business rhythm, such as board meetings, or strategic-planning processes and budget reviews.
- Prepare you for any known issues and deadlines that are likely to arise while you are out and that will require your attention.
- Prepare a dossier on the people you're meeting with on your trip, and help you think through your talking points and responses to "rude Q&A" (maybe with the help of an internal communications/PR team).
- Create a loose framework for who makes which calls in your absence, which decisions merit your being awakened in the middle of the night, and which ones can wait.

In Chapter 2, I referred to the acquisition of Washington Mutual by JPMorgan Chase in the midst of the 2008 U.S. financial crisis, and Barry Koch becoming a main point of integration between the two companies, especially in the area of anti-money laundering (AML) compliance, eventually assuming the role of AML Counsel to JP Morgan Chase's Head of AML. Diana Deen had worked for him as chief of staff for Bank Secrecy Act (BSA)/AML Enterprise Compliance at WaMu, and as he encountered many new rules, regulations, operational responsibilities, and the clash of two very different corporate cultures, he relied on her to help orchestrate compliance programs and ensure as smooth a transition as possible. On one occasion, when Koch was attending meetings at the Chase headquarters in New York, JP Morgan Chase requested over a thousand points of info for the integration of the two institutions. Deen began working feverishly across multiple teams in Seattle, New York, and other locations to ensure that the right data was pulled together, formatted appropriately, and reported to the right folks in a timely manner.

One chief of staff supported an executive who was out of the office 22 to 25 days a month, and with the executive's back-to-back meetings when he was in the office, I found no better example in my interviews of the chief of staff as "shopkeeper." According to this chief of staff, "Building trust and credibility with those who 'work in the shop' is the critical thing to making this successful. You can't position yourself on a pedestal where you are seen as pampered spy to the executive." He uses the analogy of being a distiller (versus a filter) of information, and by that he means the chief of staff shouldn't limit the flow of information between the "shop" and the executive but rather make it as efficient as possible. Also, he notes that it requires a particular skill set to manage the relationship between the chief of staff and the executive almost exclusively through email. When the executive isn't present enough to develop a deep personal relationship with, the chief of staff gets pretty good at "digital soft skills" versus traditional soft skills.

Although most examples were not as extreme as this last one, about 70 percent of chiefs of staff in my interviews performed the role of shopkeeper, to varying degrees, in their executive's absence.

## DEVELOPING AND RETAINING GOOD PEOPLE

Over the past decade and a half, leaders and organizations have increasingly focused on hiring more for an overall set of talent and potential than for one specific job. This concept has been high-lighted in numerous articles and perhaps most popularized by Marcus Buckingham and Curt Coffman's *First, Break All the Rules*.[21] You might be so busy getting the right people on the bus that you're actually not sure how to keep them engaged until you can put them in the right seat. You might also have a high-potential employee in your organization who is at the top of his or her function but who has no clear career progression beyond the current role. As roles and organization structures change with a company's evolution, you might find there are good, skilled people who don't have a clear fit in the current organization but whom you don't want to lose. Finally, ample research points to a gap in leadership talent and experience between the retiring Baby Boomer generation and Generation Y/Millennials.[22] The chief of staff role, which is most often set up as a two-to-three-year rotational position, is an attractive option for developing and keeping people engaged in any of these situations.

### Rotational chief of staff

About 50 percent of the organizations in my interviews used the chief of staff as a formal, rotational position that is specifically designed to develop high-potential leaders in the organization. In this model, the role is used to take a high-potential middle-to-senior manager out of a specific functional role and have that person learn about and participate in the whole business and all of its functions, and then "re-enter" a function as a junior executive. This was my experience in the role, as I moved from a senior manager role in sales operations into the chief of staff role, learned the business from the president and COO's perspective, and landed as a junior executive in a director of business development role. PayPal, as another example, offers future leaders exposure to environments they've never been in by rotating them through four, six-month leadership experiences (two years total), including leadership of three special projects and a rotational chief of staff position.

One opportunity this approach offers is that you have a built-in way to keep current as organizational needs change. The skill set needed in a chief of staff in year one is likely to differ greatly from that needed in year three or five. Another opportunity is that the role enables you to develop "bench depth" and get to know first-hand the relative strengths of people who will likely become your senior leaders over time. You do this by letting more talented people experience the "mini, on-the-job MBA" that the role promises. This can be especially helpful if your organization is experiencing the perceived generational gap in leadership skills and experiences, because it enables you to move more people through this fairly comprehensive and accelerated leadership (and management) training ground. According to my research, a majority of chiefs of staff moved into director-level or VP roles within one to three years after completing their tenures as chief of staff.

One challenge for this model is keeping continuity of expectations and execution. The organization, including you, has to adjust to the new chief of staff's focus (style, strengths, background) every few years. Depending on the number and complexity of other personnel changes in the organization, this can present different levels of disruption to your staff. Another challenge is that the rotational version creates a particular set of adjustments for the chief of staff to make when he or she re-enters the organization. For a detailed exploration of re-entry challenges, see Chapter 7, "Best Practices for Evolving the Role."

### Career chief of staff

About 30 percent of the organizations in my interviews used the role for long-term continuity of internal and external relationships. In this model, the same person stayed in the role for five or more years. Like the rotational version, this model poses its own opportunities and challenges.

One opportunity in the career model is that you have glue to hold the organization together during leadership transitions (see the section "Significant Changes in Leadership" in Chapter 2). Another opportunity in the long-term model is that the chief of staff role can provide a landing place for senior executives in the company who have lots of knowledge, skill, and relationships but don't want, or aren't in the running for, the top executive spots. These leaders can be great advisors to you and your staff. Some executives and chiefs of staff referred to their experience as a "sunset" position that bookended a successful career. This use of the role is akin to the elder statesman in government. One chief of staff in a Silicon Valley automotive startup said, "Even though I didn't know it at the time, I spent my career preparing for this role. This job is my reward." The elder statesman in business can also address talent development needs and generational leadership gaps by mentoring younger leaders and serving as thought partner with you and your HR head on where the talents, skills, and experience of high-potential employees can best be used in the organization.

The long-term model can also work well if you are a high-profile (maybe household) name in business, who likely has multiple financial, legal, and personal lifestyle interests, of which a particular company might be one. Someone needs to coordinate your involvement in all these interests, beyond calendars and booking travel, and the chief of staff serves more as a head of household services. One chief of staff I interviewed worked for a tech billionaire, whose interests include a great variety of scientific, humanitarian, and business ventures. "My exec wanted to build a house in Hawaii—I had to become a quick study in water rights and land-use laws to clear the permits, something completely outside the scope of work I do for the main company. Combine that with the many other projects I manage for him, and you find that as you build trust with him, he doesn't want to let you go." An executive like this doesn't want to train someone new every few years.

One more opportunity this version provides is the minimizing of disruption in the organization. Several executives and chiefs of staff indicated that once you get someone into this role and he or she does it well, you might not want to let that person go. The trusted advisor is a role that takes time to build up to, and changing that relationship when you're just getting used to someone can be particularly challenging for you and your leadership team and can disrupt results.

In this model, overall, you and the broader organization most benefit from the chief of staff's depth of relationships, depth of tribal knowledge, and historical knowledge of what's been tried before and what works and doesn't, in the current context. David Pritchard, after a number of years in technical, business management, and staffing positions at Microsoft, has served multiple executives as chief of staff for 12 years. "The job came about for me because I get along with people and have a knack for getting stuff done. In my situation, three years is great, five years is better, and longer is best because of the outside relationships that I help maintain, which are as important as the internal projects."

The main challenge of the career chief of staff is that, depending on the longevity of the executive, the chief of staff can be perceived over time to be too closely aligned with the executive and no longer able to push back on the executive or maintain that neutral stance that makes the role so valuable in the first place. Much like a writer can fail to see changes needed to content because he or she becomes too close to the content, there is danger in you and your chief of staff becoming too familiar with one another. Another challenge is that if chiefs of staff decide to re-enter the workforce in a line function, they can find that they've been typecast. Several HR executives and chiefs of staff pointed to the need for the incumbent chief of staff to stay sharp on individual skills and own some projects from beginning to end for this exact reason. One said, "While you have to be a generalist to succeed in the chief of staff role, you also can't afford to put too much weight in being a generalist because you never know when circumstances, by your choice or not, will take you out of the role and you'll need to be good at something else again."

Some executives fiercely advocated for the career model. They thought that the breadth and depth of knowledge needed to be successful is too much for the rotational version of the role. They wanted one trusted partner by their sides as their interests developed and changed. "I can't imagine 18 to 24 months for this role," said one CEO of a biotech firm. "You spend that long learning the basics of the role. It's your first time through the batting order. Becoming good at the subtleties takes time and multiple instances of similar situations to apply what you learned before in new ways.

Four or five years could be a more ideal time frame, but at least three years." Of course, much depends on the organization and leader, but it's worth noting the different schools of thought.

### The "accidental" long-term chief of staff

As I learned from about 20 percent of my interviews, the long-term model is not always intentional. The experience of Chris Adams at Direct Line Insurance reflected that of some others I spoke to. He had intended to serve in a chief of staff role for a couple years when he got paired up with new CEO Paul Geddes during Direct Line's spinoff from RBS. Five years later, he moved on to a director-level HR position in leadership development. Adams says his five years was probably not ideal. He felt stale by the end of it, as he and the exec were finishing each other's sentences and had arguably become more alike than the complementary model they thought was most effective.

In my earlier discussion of the history of the role, I covered the unlikely event of betrayal by a chief of staff. If this conflict is a concern for you or others in the organization, then the rotational model could be the most suitable, because it normally draws on a more junior, further-removed talent from your position; such an individual is less likely to be a succession threat. In addition, the rotational model allows less time for the chief of staff to fully realize your complete range of strengths and weaknesses than the longer-term model.

If you've kept track of the math, you've noticed that the rotational and long-term models I've mentioned so far constitute only 80 percent of chiefs of staff. In the remaining 20 percent, the chief of staff was intended for a short stint (less than 36 months) but turned into a long-term role (three to five years or longer) that either became a rotational program later or evolved into a career position. In theory, a chief of staff role could be set up, serve its function, and then be dissolved, but I did not find any examples of this in my research. To the contrary, once an executive used a chief of staff, he or she usually continued to use the role.

---

## ◼ REFLECT & APPLY

After looking at the second pivot, reported benefits of the chief of staff role, I offer the following questions for assessment and reflection:

**1.** Use this circle to create a pie chart as appropriate:

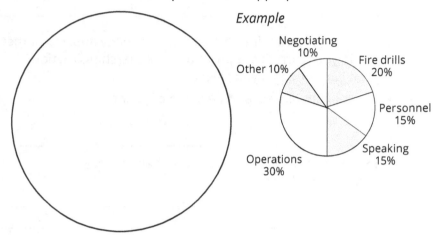

*Example*

**2.** What percent of your time would you *like* to spend on each of the categories above?

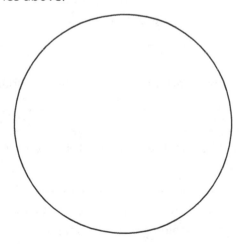

**3.** What do you make of any gaps between how you spend your time today and how you'd like to? Would a chief of staff help you close the gaps? Why or why not?

_____

_____

_____

_____

**4.** Of the reported benefits of the role, how many apply to unmet needs in your current organization or leadership situation? Explain each one that you select.

- Focusing on highest and best use of your time

_____

_____

- Executing or overseeing work that has no clear departmental owner

_____

_____

- Knowing what's really going on

_____

_____

- Making and executing great decisions

_____

_____

- Shortening your learning curve in a new company or industry

_____

_____

- Resting assured that the business functions when you are away

_____

_____

- Developing and retaining good people

_____

_____

**5.** Knowing what you know now, how do you see a chief of staff helping with these unmet needs? Be specific (for example, you think your team make good decisions, but implementing those decisions is where your organization needs help).

_____

_____

_____

_____

## RHYTHM/CADENCE OF THE BUSINESS

You want to set and maintain an appropriate pace of board and leadership meetings, as well as check-ins with your internal and external stakeholders. This involves driving the structure, content, and timely execution of a number of things:

- Investor and board meetings
- Staff meetings (group)
- 1:1 meetings with staff and founders/board members
- All-hands meetings
- Business reviews/internal governance meetings
- Planning processes related to operations, strategy, human capital (with budget presumably coming from the CFO)
- Training and team building (initial and sustainment)
- Morale events

Chiefs of staff and business managers most commonly do the legwork for these, because it frees you to focus on your highest and best use of your time. In the section on "Making and Executing Great Decisions" in Chapter 3, I described some of the work a chief of staff does in preparing you for these meetings, but a lot of the work is in partnering with you to form the rhythm of these meetings, based on the chief of staff's exposure to your overall goals for the organization and how the leadership team are making progress toward those goals.

One executive I interviewed noted the time when she and her staff discovered that monthly leadership team meetings weren't working. She and the staff rarely got to the agenda items they wanted to discuss, because the monthly meeting was their only formal touchpoint, as a team, before a monthly meeting with the board. Consequently the monthly leadership team meeting was inadvertently being driven by only the topics that would be covered in board meetings. Yet they needed to work on so much more. So the chief of staff presented a range of options, from a daily huddle concept to a biweekly cadence (the eventual "winner"). They shifted the frequency and format of the leadership team meeting, put tight guidelines around the submission of materials before the meeting so that the actual meeting time was focused on substantive issues, and began covering the topics they needed to.

You might wonder why this rhythm isn't best handled by your executive assistant. It's a good question, and I explore the differences between the chief of staff and the EA in more depth in Chapter 5. Most of the people I interviewed, including EAs, noted that EAs tend to help executives schedule the meeting, prepare meeting materials, schedule any pre-meeting conversations if needed, and prepare the room with food or audiovisual equipment. But it was the chief of staff who helped the executive to decide on the agenda and what materials would be needed for the meeting, in what format; to pre-negotiate outcomes so that the big decision meeting was a formality or last chance to raise concerns. In the meeting itself, some executives used an EA to take minutes and record what was being said, but the chief of staff was more likely to have not only the senior leader's authority and cachet with the leadership team but also the business experience and political savvy to interrupt, challenge, and question even the top boss, as needed, with broad business perspectives and strategic goals in mind. Even in cases in which the EA was given the chief of staff title or responsibilities, he or she was better respected as a substantive contributor to the conversation if a more senior partner was present to back up the EA.

At the highest level of the organization, a chief of staff partners with you to set the agendas and pace of these events and meetings. Further into the organization, you might have a chief of staff or business manager who ensures that his or her team's rhythms mirror those of the broader organization and enable the timely delivery of any inputs they have to those events and meetings.

## COMMUNICATIONS

The chief of staff helps you manage the following aspects of your communication:

- An effective information network
- Presentations/speaking engagements to a variety of audiences
- Meeting preparation
- Written communications to internal and external stakeholders (up, down, and outside the organization)
- Organization announcements

You need an effective information network—providing an ear to the ground to know what's going on up and down the organization and outside the organization (investors, customers, press), and listening to constituent concerns and partnering in problem solving/creating solutions (see the section "Knowing What's Really Going On in Your Organization" in Chapter 3).

You also need to prepare and deliver presentations and speaking engagements for investors, boards, C-level execs, staff, direct reports, and external parties such as industry associations, conferences, and the college graduation ceremony at which you've been invited to speak. The chief of staff helps you maintain clear and consistent themes, messages, and delivery across venues. Almost universally, executives reported that they relied on the chief of staff to remind them what they had said in previous meetings, to ensure that they weren't sending mixed signals or, if they had sent mixed signals, that they clarified as soon as possible.

The chief of staff also runs interference (with the EA) on your calendar, blocks time, and ensures that you have time for grounding yourself for (especially high-profile) speaking engagements. Whether you are preparing for an important speaking engagement, a meeting, a discussion, or a decision, the chief of staff plays a role in getting you into an appropriate frame of mind by asking questions such as these:

- If it's your meeting, what tone do you want to set? What are the themes and emotional appeals you are going for?
- If it's someone else's meeting, what is being requested of you and what data or political dynamics in the room should you be mindful of going into the meeting?

## UNIVERSAL COMPETENCIES

### Anticipation

In Chapters 1 and 5, I describe the systems and process thinking competency, and it is precisely that orientation that leads a chief of staff to accurately and successfully anticipate needs and problems in the organization and help you get ahead of them. Additional insights from my interviews include these:

- A chief of staff has to anticipate risks and deal in contingencies. He or she prepares you not just with a plan B but with plans C, D, and E.
- A chief of staff must make recommendations for future actions based on learning from history. See the "$50 Million Question" anecdote in the Introduction.
- A chief of staff doesn't wait for a big meeting to make decisions. He or she pre-negotiates outcomes through "sneaker diplomacy," closed-door conversations, and management by walking around.
- Whether it's spotting a need to improve communication between geographically dispersed groups or telling a household-name leader that he has spinach in his teeth, a chief of staff doesn't wait for permission to act but takes initiative.

"When my chief of staff was helping me orchestrate a restructuring with some layoffs," one president says, "of course he worked with HR, legal, and communications, but without my asking him, he set up special channels of communication for people who had questions and also set about coaching the remaining people through the change and disruption to their work and lives. He even worked on his own time to have coffee and happy hours with some of the people laid off, to point them to resources that might be helpful to them."

- What are some tactical discussions you might need to have behind closed doors before you get to the strategic conversation you want?
- Have you established and rehearsed talking points around key items that might come up?
- Do you have clear and consistent themes, messages, and delivery across venues?

entirely different person. The bad news is, it's hard to find a template for success that you can apply if you're creating the role from scratch. There are no "three easy steps" to finding the ideal chief of staff candidate. The good news is, the absence of a formal definition is also the opportunity for each executive to custom-craft the role to his or her unique circumstances or business needs. Finally, even though your HR partner will identify people and help with a lot of the sourcing, screening, and interviewing legwork, you can only partner to the extent that you've thought about and answered some of the issues and questions in this section for yourself.

Executives use chiefs of staff from a variety of functional backgrounds, such as speech writing, project management, operations analysis, and strategic or financial planning. Although chiefs of staff perform many roles, they often focus in a particular area, based on the functional area they came from or a particular people skill that they possess. Nearly half of my interview respondents mentioned something along the lines of being hired to bring EQ— emotional intelligence—to a high-IQ organization, for example. The answer to what emphasis you need lies in where your biggest gaps are. One or more focus areas might have become evident to you in reading the previous chapters, and I include here some additional considerations.

## TYPICAL PIVOTS FOR DETERMINING EMPHASIS

Based on the needs you identified while deciding to hire for this role, the emphasis for the chief of staff role might have become clear. If not, you can ask some questions that might help you narrow it down (see the "Reflect and Apply" worksheet at the end of this chapter for more space to make notes):

- *Will your chief of staff be rotational or long-term?* (See "Developing and Retaining Good People" in Chapter 3.)
- *What level of rank and experience will your chief of staff need to have?* We've discussed how a chief of staff can span the

ranks from "executive assistant plus" to vice president. (See "What Is a Chief of Staff?" in Chapter 1.) An estimated 80 percent of corporate chiefs of staff have at least six to eight years of professional experience, and 60 percent have 10 or more years of experience.[1]

- *Will your chief of staff be a generalist or a specialist? Or, what blend of technical expertise/task orientation or people/relational orientation will you require?* For example, if you are a CFO, do you really need another financial analyst, or do you need someone with an operational or a people management emphasis? If you are head of a technical function, do you need someone who knows the inner workings of your technology and your team or someone who brings an outsider perspective? (See "The Leader's Strengths" in Chapter 2.)

- *What mix of thought partner and doer do your business needs require?* (See "Leaders with Particular Styles, Strengths, and Positions" in Chapter 2.)

- *How much time do you spend away from headquarters?* Someone who is away more often requires someone with what one chief of staff termed "digital soft skills." Arguably, a more senior chief of staff will have more influence while you are away, whereas your presence might lend more weight to a junior chief of staff's requests of your team.

- *What's the rhythm of reporting in your organization, and who sets it?* If you're in a heavily regulated industry, you might hire a fact-checker or someone who can enforce compliance mandates. If you're in a tech company where regular reporting on key performance indicators (KPIs) is of primary importance, you might hire someone with an analytics or operations background who knows what needs to be reported and can pull it together from multiple parts of the business for the CEO, board, or investors. My interviews suggested that not only can a chief of staff help

Nicole Grogan, who as a senior HR executive has managed chiefs of staff, their executives, or both at Allied Signal, Cisco, and Intellectual Ventures, puts it this way:

> I have worked in situations where the executive has a very strong, educated, or experienced EA who understood the business and performed most duties assumed by a chief of staff with a more junior admin professional reporting to him/her that enabled him/her to scale to the broader set of responsibilities.... In situations where the exec has a very strong admin team and ops leader, the chief of staff can be less necessary.

The EA as chief of staff tends to work well when coupled with a more senior operations leader and can be better suited to an executive whose need is more tactical (following up on action items from key meetings, ensuring time lines are met, scheduling meetings with the executive in the event of an escalation). From a talent development standpoint, this role can be a great career growth opportunity for an EA who wants to move into positions with greater responsibility over time (see "The Ambitious Executive Assistant" later in this chapter).

On the other hand, the vice president as chief of staff can work best if the business need of the supported executive is much more visionary, strategic, or requires someone with seniority and the weight of formal authority in the organization to inspire and drive teams toward a common goal. Several executives noted that the EA, right or wrong, is not likely to command the same level of respect that the VP will in complex, cross-departmental initiatives, especially if there is entrenched conflict or political jockeying. Given EAs' traditional involvement in routine, predictable tasks, some also questioned whether most EAs could tolerate and successfully navigate ambiguity at the level required for the chief of staff role. As one chief of staff from a large U.S. services firm says, "You can abruptly change from heading north to heading east in this role. How will you move fast enough without having all the answers?" A senior manager/VP-level employee is more likely to have the experience of leading people through ambiguous situations, while maintaining executive presence and demonstrating the political savvy to remove systemic roadblocks that get in the way of what he or she has been tasked with.

To this point about experience and credibility, I spoke to a handful of people who began their careers as EAs and later served as chiefs of staff, sometimes (but not always) for the same executive they had served as EA. Having a couple steps beyond the EA position under their belt seems to have better positioned them for the chief of staff role. Tara Lappin at Cisco served as an EA to an executive VP before eventually landing in the chief of staff role. She describes her evolution this way:

> Everything that executive VP approved went through me. I didn't have the power to make decisions for him but knew what he was looking for. From there, I went into IT management, first in managing contracts and then programs. In 2010, my executive sponsor said I'd make a good chief of staff, even though I had no idea what it was. By the end of the day, I was talking to a VP of infrastructure, whose COS was going on leave and who wondered if I'd take the job. I already had several years' experience with him, had good rapport, and had built up trust.

You will likely call upon your chief of staff to perform in situations dramatic and mundane, strategic and tactical. For many, this is the attraction of the position. As one chief of staff put it, "One minute I was negotiating a nine-figure deal and the next minute I was booking my boss's rental car. You don't get to negotiate nine-figure deals at my age and experience level without taking some of the good with the bad. It's easy to come out of the nine-figure deal meeting and think you're too close to the boss to work on the little things like signing expense reports, but it's just not true of this role—you do what it takes."

Doing what it takes is simply a matter of trade-offs. If setting up easels and white boards for a planning session is what is required, you don't want a chief of staff to say something like, "Well, that's the EA's job." It might very well be the EA's job, but if the EA isn't

## UNIVERSAL COMPETENCIES

### Adaptability and flexibility

I describe adaptability and flexibility to some extent in "Universal Competencies" in this chapter. Additional insights from my interviews include these:

- A chief of staff needs to be able to operate in the strategic world one minute, tactical the next, or shift from topic to topic in rapid succession.

- A chief of staff might be in the background for a large part of a meeting but needs to pay close attention so that he or she can recall detailed information when called on to do so.

- A chief of staff can't be so attached to formal processes and methodologies, or by-the-book ways of doing things, that he or she misses opportunities to be resourceful.

One CEO says, "Formally certified project managers can struggle in this role, because if I want a plan, it takes time for them to scope the tasks, do a detailed work breakdown structure (WBS), figure out all task dependencies, plan the resources, determine a time line and milestones, and get buy-in from stakeholders. Those are all important, but it's too late. I'd rather have a 60–70 percent, good enough plan, quickly, then add all that once we are moving forward on the work."

in the room, the chief of staff becomes the chief-get-it-done officer in the room. You won't learn about these kinds of trade-offs in business school, because the exact nature of them can't be predicted. You need someone who can figure it out when previous templates won't apply.

## UNIVERSAL COMPETENCIES

Similar to the need to consider the pivot on deliverables, you need a chief of staff with multiple competencies for the role to succeed, and the difference between a CEO's needs and a department/function head's needs lies in the emphasis and focus of these competencies. Of course, there are some baseline competencies that you'd expect any of your leaders to have—problem-solving ability, communication skills, and functional competence in one or more areas; but from my interviews I identified the following combination of competencies that chiefs of staff tended to demonstrate in large measure:

- *Results orientation*—The ability not just to manage work until it's complete but also to measure success afterward and make adjustments in future work.
- *Systems and process thinking*—Using systems and processes to manage and measure work; understanding organizational dynamics and structure and the systemic advantages and disadvantages inherent in them.
- *Anticipation*—Forward thinking and understanding where the industry, your company, and you are headed; accurately connecting the dots between disparate parts of the organization. This also includes anticipating your individual needs—do you need a dossier on the other party in an upcoming meeting, what info do you need in it, etc.?
- *Political savvy*—Understanding formal and informal power in the organization and how to use these to further your vision or get work done.
- *Coaching*—Questioning assumptions or challenging the status quo; helping others see what they haven't yet seen; asking powerful questions that expand others' thinking or feelings; understanding resistance to change in the organization and helping individuals and teams work through it.
- *Managed ego or servant leadership*—The ability to balance the positional power that the chief of staff wields and his or her personal influence in the organization to reach the outcomes that you are seeking.
- *Adaptability and flexibility*—The ability to shift gears rapidly from one subject to another, multiple times a day; to weather change; to tolerate and successfully navigate ambiguity; and to demonstrate resourcefulness.
- *Interpretation or translation*—Helping others understand your vision so that they can act, and helping you understand others' vision and problems so you can make better decisions.

FIGURE 5.3   Chief of Staff Competencies, by Leader's Position*

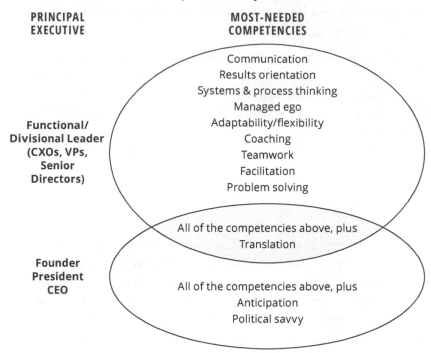

| PRINCIPAL EXECUTIVE | MOST-NEEDED COMPETENCIES |
|---|---|

Functional/ Divisional Leader (CXOs, VPs, Senior Directors)

Communication
Results orientation
Systems & process thinking
Managed ego
Adaptability/flexibility
Coaching
Teamwork
Facilitation
Problem solving

All of the competencies above, plus
Translation

Founder
President
CEO

All of the competencies above, plus
Anticipation
Political savvy

*with contributions by Collen Hunter, Vivian Mason, and Slalom Consulting

Obviously some competencies will depend on your situation. If your chief of staff will manage people or have substantive input on HR decisions, for example, people development or hiring might be important competencies for you to consider. Figure 5.3 shows the competencies that are generally most important for various categories of leaders.

## COMMON PERSONALITY PROFILES

During my interviews, a lot of people asked me if I had found a common personality or work profile among the individuals who are attracted to the chief of staff role. Late in my research, I began to test this question. I wanted to see whether successful chiefs of staff exhibited certain personality traits, skills, or strengths based on popular assessments, such as the Myers-Briggs Type Indicator® (MBTI®), Hogan, DiSC®, Insights, StrengthsFinder, and so forth.

In terms of personality profiles, the most common assessment that chiefs of staff had taken was MBTI. Based on that, I took a look at the distribution of types to see what I could find. (In case you're not familiar with them, "types" in MBTI are based on preferences in four dichotomies: Extraversion or Introversion [E or I], Sensing or Intuition [S or I], Thinking or Feeling [T or F], and Judging or Perceiving [J or P].) The vast majority of chiefs of staff surveyed fell into the Guardians or Idealists categories; there were no Artisans and few Rationals. People with the ESTJ profile led the field (25 percent), with ISTJ, INFJ, and ENFP coming in second (17 percent each). Last were the ESFJ, INFP, and INTJ (8 percent each). This is an area that I have begun to research in more depth, and I hope to publish more conclusive data and findings in a revision of this book or online content in the near future.

## WHERE TO LOOK FOR YOUR CHIEF OF STAFF

Once you have determined the emphasis for your chief of staff, you can (alone or working with your HR partner), start looking for someone in (or outside) the organization who falls into one or more of these categories:

- Has a reputation for "getting stuff done" or making order out of chaos.
- Has been identified by your talent development program for, and has a desire to pursue, a fast track to more senior roles, including the executive ranks.
- Has worked with you on projects before and earned your trust through his or her competence and ethics.
- Possesses a disparate/eclectic skill and experience set that gives him or her an advantage over deep experts in a single function or specialty.
- Is an executive assistant with the desire and business experience to expand his or her responsibility beyond the

traditional EA activities of scheduling, filing, and concierge services.

- Is transitioning from a military or governmental chief of staff role to the corporate sector.

- Is transitioning from a consulting company to a product company.

### The person who gets stuff done

In the film adaptation of Lauren Weisberger's *The Devil Wears Prada*, we find a young executive assistant fielding the impossible demands of her boss. "Where's that piece of paper I had in my hand yesterday morning?" "Pick up my shoes from Blahnik, and then go get Patricia." (Who's that?) "Get me that little table that I liked at that store on Madison." "Get us a reservation for dinner tonight at that place that got the good review."[4] Likewise, your chief of staff probably needs to be adept at translating even the most incomprehensible, or unreasonable, requests into action, making sure it's the right action, and testing the outputs of the action to ensure that what was promised by the organization is what gets delivered.

As I've noted earlier in this book, the chief of staff serves as the connective tissue or translational capability between you and the rest of the organization. Think of Amanda Mancuso at SCYNEXIS being the one that the staff go to for clarification and follow-up on Yves Ribeill's vision (see "Managing Projects and Change, and Coaching" in Chapter 3). Having a chief of staff who excels in this translational capability helps you focus on your highest and best use of your time because that person, not you, spends the time needed for clarifying, and it prevents the chief of staff from being seen by the rest of the organization as a wedge between you and your staff because good outcomes (among other things) establish trust.

The need for someone who simply gets stuff done is one reason so many executives lean on a chief of staff from a project management or program management background. Such individuals don't need formal training, but they have to demonstrate street smarts when it comes to delivering projects on time and on budget. In fact, some executives and chiefs of staff I spoke with argued that focusing on formal processes too much can hinder the organization's ability to be flexible and change direction when change dictates it. One executive said, "I asked one of my department heads for action to be taken on an issue we were having. The formal project management folks in that department said they'd come back to their leader and me in a couple weeks—it would take them that long to interview stakeholders, identify key milestones and time lines, figure out the resourcing, identify risks, and develop a risk mitigation plan. My chief of staff sketched out a plan by the next morning that was good enough. If I had been asking for a major cultural shift, the former might have worked, but we were bleeding money in this problem area, and two weeks would've cost us more than it was worth."

Another nuanced aspect of getting stuff done is keeping an eye on tasks that go undone over time. Some tasks go undone because they aren't important. Some tasks aren't yours to do. Credit yourself with good prioritization and delegation skills for those. Others, however, don't start as high priority by themselves, but if they go unaddressed over time, they can actually block your initiatives and take on critical-path status or a higher priority over time. Tracking these is not likely the highest and best use of your time. A good chief of staff can be someone in your organization who serves as the early warning system for those tasks that are growing in priority and, having previously gone largely unnoticed, need to be dealt with.

In Chapter 2, I quoted Chris Briggs of Providence Health & Services as saying, "It takes a special skill set to bridge what needs to happen at the staff level and what needs to happen at the executive level." He adds, "The executive is looking forward to where her function is going in the future, or looking to the CEO for cues on where the markets are taking the entire organization. It's the chief of staff's job, mostly, to look back and kind of pull the staff along, to help them get on board with where we're headed and to focus on the tactical and operational things that we need to do to get us where we want to go."

## "High potentials" from your talent development program

Al Chase makes the claim that "a typical pattern for the rotational chief of staff (versus the career chief of staff) is to learn the ropes by serving alongside a CEO and learning how a C-suite executive operates before joining the executive ranks, too."[5] The chief of staff role is not a guaranteed fast track to anywhere. But many chiefs of staff experience the role as a path, even a shortcut, to the executive ranks.

In my research, I focused not only on where chiefs of staff came from before taking the position but also where they went afterward. Although not all chiefs of staff follow a set career progression, some trends and tendencies were evident. Chiefs of staff tend to move into senior leadership positions in the same company, often taking on significant P&L responsibilities and increased numbers of direct reports. A notable example is Avani Saglani Davda, who moved into a CEO role for Tata Starbucks as the coffee chain opened its first store in Mumbai in 2012.[6] Looking at one data set of approximately 68,000 worldwide, past and present chiefs of staff (excluding government, military, and specific medical versions of the role), about 10,000 (15 percent) eventually became CXO of a public company; about 8,400 (12.5 percent) became vice presidents; about 4,200 (6 percent) started their own company; and 1,233 (2 percent) became partners in consulting, law, or private practices of various sorts. In short, about a third of people who have served as a chief of staff in the past are currently sitting at or near the top of their respective worlds. If you count the additional 12,000 (18 percent) who are in director-level positions or above, a little over half of all chiefs of staff end up in the executive ranks after their tenure. In many instances, they held their top positions within one to three years of departure from the chief of staff role, but the data are not available to draw any solid conclusions as to a precise time frame it takes for one to advance from chief of staff to executive. If you're wondering about the remaining 46 percent, they were still serving in the role, were less than one to three years removed from their time in the role, had taken lateral moves to learn the ropes in a new function, or were already at a director-level or higher rank in the organization when they took the chief of staff role.

And why not? Chiefs of staff should be well suited for promotion because they come to know so much about the business, enjoy numerous and deep relationships with people in powerful positions, and have experienced what some call a mini-MBA through on-the-job training. There is arguably no other role that pulls your high-potential people out of a department- or function-specific job such as sales, finance, or operations; creates a new vantage point across all departments and functions; establishes them as leaders across groups; and then places them back into the business with the strength of their improved knowledge of the company's products, people, processes, and politics. This is precisely why for you and your HR executives, the chief of staff position can be a great option for developing high-potential talent, creating bench depth, and developing a deep succession plan at multiple layers in the organization.

In many companies, talent development seems to mean "grow up or grow out." If you don't have ambition to climb the ladder on a management track, you get managed out. Companies figure you've reached your maximum potential under the Peter Principle. For the brave souls who raise their hands and say, "But I like being an individual contributor," many companies aren't quite sure what to do with that. Not everyone wants to be at the top, and not everyone in your organization might fit neatly into your talent development framework. You might have seasoned individual contributors in your organization who are looking for a stretch assignment. Or, as several chiefs of staff noted, you don't often see a White House chief of staff become a U.S. president, because they actually like and might be better suited to being in the number-two spot, behind the scenes—more vice president, less president. One chief of staff put it this way: "I was born a chief of staff. It just took me 40 years to understand it. I refer to this as leading from the middle. Having no authority, per se, but influencing the people around you to accomplish something. At home, I was a middle child between two generations of kids. At school I was in positions between my peer group and teachers/faculty. And early in my career I worked in public relations, employee communications, and human resources, where I was between employees and management. Some people feel cramped in the middle (like the middle seat on an airplane). I feel energized there." Another chief of staff found that the job offered a crystal ball through which he could see himself in his boss's role someday; but after seeing the demands on his boss's time from so many directions (between work, home, charity activities, and requests for speaking engagements), he concluded that climbing the ladder actually seemed less appealing from a personal motivation standpoint. He believed that you can't have it all, and he made his choice not to go down that road. You might have the sunset careerist that I mentioned in "Developing and Retaining Good People" in Chapter 3. The chief of staff role might keep engaged, talented, and experienced people in your organization who could otherwise get washed out.

### The person who's earned your trust in past projects

The extent to which a candidate has previously worked with you is one indicator of potential success in the role. Past experience with one another is not a prerequisite for success, however. In my interviews (as opposed to the broader set of 68,000 people mentioned above), the largest single group (44 percent) moved from a part of the company, or from another industry or geographic location, where they had had no exposure to the executive or the staff. Twenty-two percent had not had direct experience with each other, but the chief of staff had worked with at least one department head and came with strong recommendations. However, one-third (the second-largest group) *did* have prior experience with their executives, which makes it a point worth considering.

Having prior experience with an eventual chief of staff hire can reduce the amount of effort required by you or your staff to build or maintain trust with that person in the early days of his or her tenure. Most of the chiefs of staff in that one-third group had demonstrated through performance and trust that they were worth actively seeking for the role. One chief of staff said, "I first got to know the boss and delivered high-value projects for her early in my career—seven years later, she was managing director of a large bank division, and she looked for a way to get me in because we had a history of trust. That's how I landed in the chief of staff role."

## The business generalist who offers more than a deep expert in a single field

As I've noted previously in this book, a chief of staff role might require varying degrees of specialization or generalization. Even if the chief of staff serves a technical role, he or she would not likely be in the role if not for the demonstrated ability to take multiple aspects of day-to-day management off your desk.

Generally, in a technical assistant version of the role, you might find that a technical background carries more weight. At a software company, for example, someone from a general marketing background can be focused on offering more customized products to a wider market, whereas someone with a specific engineering focus is more concerned with how a particular product or product line can be more standardized. Someone with a technical marketing background or a former developer or tester who now manages programs—a business generalist with experience in multiple aspects of the business—will, better than people in any single function, understand the engineering and marketing trade-offs involved in getting software products to market and will serve you and your staff better as a result.

If you're a functional head who is using a business manager or a business operations manager version of the role, you're more likely to succeed finding someone from a project or program management, business analyst, or finance function.

Most of the job descriptions you see for the chief of staff role include verbiage about "broad business experience." Al Chase, in his *Chief of Staff—A Force Multiplier!* white paper, highlights some of the functional competencies of chiefs of staff and then adds, "Wow! We just described Superman or Wonder Woman."[7] You might wonder if any such person exists. From my work, I know that at least 68,000 of these people do exist in the business world, and that does not include an additional 16,000 to 20,000 people in the military or governmental versions of the role.

Keith Naber, a chief of staff at Intel, cautions chiefs of staff against being too much of a generalist. "The ones I've seen succeed in the chief of staff role stood on their own, too. They were excellent in a function, whether finance, operations management, and so forth." His caution seems wise, especially from the chief of staff's point of view. According to one HR executive, "Considering and deciding whether you want a specialist or a generalist is one of the most important steps you can take. The types of assignments your chief of staff might excel at or move into beyond his or her tenure in your office can very much be influenced by this." If your chief of staff comes to the role with a strength in one area and isn't necessarily an expert in other areas, then he or she can more easily decide what kinds of work to delegate or get help with. For example, he or she might be great at financial analysis but hand off draft communications to the communications team, or vice versa.

### The ambitious executive assistant

In the section "Titles and Why They Matter" earlier in this chapter, I provide a continuum that shows a range of responsibilities that tend to distinguish executive assistants (EAs) from other roles, such as vice presidents. I also make the point that, right or wrong, senior leaders can have a bias against EAs as chiefs of staff because of the perception that EAs lack the experience, credibility, and sophistication to play the game of business at their level. In many cases, this can be true. Yet I also discussed in that same section how an EA as chief of staff can succeed with the proper scoping and support.

One thing that I noticed while interviewing EAs for a former boss was that the higher up in an organization you go, the more types of functions an EA seems likely to perform, even beyond the traditional scope of the EA role. For example, many of the EAs I interviewed managed board meetings for their executives, even to the level of providing a point of view on the executive's themes and messaging in the meeting, and taking on many of the responsibilities I attributed to the chief of staff as meeting manager in "Analyzing and Framing Decisions" in Chapter 3. So an assumption that

EAs work only on a very narrowly defined set of tasks is already tentative.

You might find an EA who used to occupy higher-ranked jobs—even management jobs—in the past but chose the EA role for a variety of career or personal reasons. Some EAs have project management certificates or business degrees, and many can knock out the work on the routine side of the continuum in 40 to 50 percent of their day, leaving a lot of bandwidth for handling more complex matters. These EAs might end up taking on special projects, tracking action items for the executive team, and serving as leaders for other EAs. These are not "just" traditional EAs. They are more akin to chiefs of staff than many observers would like to believe.

Todd Dunham, who goes by the title of Corporate Operations Assistant, worked as an EA to the CEO of American Airlines Federal Credit Union before coming to Brooks Sports as EA to the CFO. He described his evolution to his current chief of staff role this way:

> As an EA for the CFO of a smaller company, I had the opportunity to come into Brooks as an EA on a contract basis. We developed the position to support the SVP of HR and CFO in expanding the admin network, allowing them to focus on fewer administrative tasks. Now I work on a combination of special projects and ongoing operations, which involves a lot of coordination between our HQ in Seattle and our global offices in Asia and Europe. I try to bring greater efficiency for the executives, ensure that they control their calendars and enable them to be proactive. During a major internal re-alignment, I coordinated the executives on some cross-departmental work, ensuring all the right players had effective lines of communication, were in the right meetings, and so forth.
>
> Recently, a facility manager was taking sabbatical while moving our HQ into a new building that was in the certification process for a green building. With no apparent backfill while she was gone, I took the lead and represented our interests in the building certification process, light programing, energy usage, rain water collection cistern for use in toilets, etc. and working with contractors to ensure we got what we had asked for.

You might find that the ambitious EA has what it takes to succeed in a chief of staff role. EAs who've served senior leaders in a company already have some exposure and relationship with you and your staff, and might understand the politics between groups and how to get things done, even though to date they might have only done so at the tactical level. You likely already trust your EA with confidential information and believe that he or she will know what to say to whom, when. Your EA might have sat in on certain meetings as a minute-taker and have more business context for what is going on than one who simply caters lunch for the meeting and disappears. Your EA likely has relationships throughout the business by way of serving you, relationships that can be used effectively in a chief of staff function. If your EA has managed special projects for you, such as making sure the company's annual goal-setting process is completed in partnership with HR, you can trust him or her to run special projects as your chief of staff. In this situation, you might give that person additional responsibility as a way to test his or her limits. You might also use that individual in conjunction with another senior leader to jointly carry out chief of staff tasks. You and your staff might be surprised at how well he or she performs. The EA candidate will likely have to work harder than most to demonstrate an ability to play the business game at the strategic level, show the requisite level of political savvy, and be a thought partner to you. But if you have a strong EA candidate, hiring that person can save you time and effort on sourcing and recruiting, and the chief of staff role can be a great tool for developing and keeping him or her engaged.

As I noted in the "Titles and Why They Matter" section, you might also find someone a step or two removed from the EA role as a way around the perception of experience and creditability issues. A candidate with other high-level strategy or operating experience will command a certain amount of respect from your team out of the gate.

You have some things to think about in this scenario, but it's worth considering.

## The military or governmental chief of staff

The chief of staff role can be a great stepping-stone for people who want to transition from their military or government careers to the civilian workforce. As one chief of staff said, "Washington, D.C., is the place ideas go to die. Just as some folks get burned out on corporate life and rotate into government out of a sense of giving back and being part of something bigger than themselves, I was a little burned out on D.C. and wanted to work where ideas were being generated, so I looked at and eventually settled here in a hotbed city for high tech."

Because the role tends to favor generalists over specialists, looking at the military and at government institutions can help you find outsiders who might bring fresh thinking and insight to those with a specialty or deep expertise in your company's core business. The risk of this scenario is that the chief of staff faces a steep learning curve to become expert in the specifics of the business. How quickly could he or she learn pricing models, or the particulars of your pricing models? Does it matter for your situation?

One chief of staff I interviewed had served as deputy chief of staff in a U.S. government agency during the Deepwater Horizon disaster, then as chief of staff to a U.S. senator before transitioning to the corporate world to serve as chief of staff to a visionary technology and business leader. He oversaw some of that leader's business at his main company but also his "hobby" scientific work, publications, and speaking engagements in diverse areas. His role included many functions similar to those of a head of a family office, a common chief-of-staff-like role for (usually very wealthy) people with multiple legal, financial, and lifestyle interests.

Another served in a chief of staff function of the United States Patent and Trademark Office (USPTO) before landing a role in a technology company for whom licensing was a major revenue stream. He went from serving the USPTO on strategic planning, policy, political issues, and operations to serving his new company's founder and vice chairman in a similar capacity.

## The consultant who wants to transition to a product company

In addition to demonstrated project management abilities (see the earlier section on "The person who gets stuff done"), several of the folks I interviewed noted that consultants often make great chiefs of staff because of several factors. First, they've likely worked on a variety of projects, often at the same time, and so they can become a quick study in many client companies or industries, or specific topics within an industry, and shift gears between them on a given day. Second, by succeeding in consulting, they've demonstrated some degree of intellectual horsepower, creativity, and problem-solving ability. Third, consulting often exposes the consultant to executives, their decision making, and their operating challenges on a day-in, day-out basis. Finally, to succeed in consulting, a candidate has most likely demonstrated an ability to listen and assess before jumping to action.

## ■ REFLECT & APPLY

After looking at your role in finding and hiring the right chief of staff (or replacement chief of staff if you've already got one), I offer the following questions for reflection and application:

1. What are your thoughts on each of the pivots for determining emphasis in this chapter?

   - Will the role be rotational or long-term?
   - What level of rank and experience will your chief of staff need to have?
   - Do you need a generalist or a specialist?
   - Do you need someone who is technically oriented, relationally oriented, or both?
   - What mix of thought partner and doer is required?
   - What percentage of your time do you spend away from headquarters?
   - What area of expertise is most important—analytics, operations, compliance (for reporting)?

   Other thoughts:

   _____

   _____

   _____

   _____


2. Do your organization dynamics, your perceived benefits from the chief of staff role, or the deliverables that you're responsible for suggest an emphasis?

   _____

   _____

   _____

   _____

3. Rank the universal competencies described in this chapter, or add your own:

| Competency | Importance |
|---|---|
| Results orientation | |
| Systems and process thinking | |
| Anticipation | |
| Political savvy | |
| Coaching | |
| Managed ego or servant leadership | |
| Adaptability and flexibility | |
| Interpretation or translation | |
| Other: | |
| Other: | |
| Other: | |

4. If you're going to spend the next two to five years or more with a chief of staff, what are some areas you most want your HR partner to screen for in interviews? Circle or numerically rank the ones I've provided, or add your own:

- The candidate thrives on fielding poorly thought-out or even completely unreasonable ideas and turning them into action.

- The candidate is okay missing a kid's recital, dinner with a significant other, or the first day of vacation or has support outside work for the time commitment.

- The candidate has the emotional wherewithal to orchestrate layoffs that involve peers and colleagues.

- The candidate excels at speaking on behalf of or drafting written communication for an influential executive (remember David Pritchard's admonition in Chapter 2 about shifting the stock markets).

- The candidate takes initiative.

- The candidate can take the heat when plans don't work out, make adjustments, and keep moving (i.e., the candidate has a thick skin).

- The candidate has been at your company, or at least in the industry, long enough to know its ins and outs.
- Other:

  _____

  _____

- Other:

  _____

  _____

# SO, YOU'VE GOT A CHIEF OF STAFF. NOW WHAT?

to even the chief of staff's most thoughtful analysis and critique. A lack of confidence between the chief of staff and your direct reports can show up as the staff doing "end runs" around the chief of staff; not opening up with their real thoughts, feelings, and values in critical meetings; and keeping your valued representative out of the loop on important discussions. In short, a lack of trust can quickly erode many of the advantages that you hired a chief of staff for in the first place. Setting expectations is the first step in the trust-building process.

In the early going, the relationship between you and your chief of staff or your chief of staff and your direct reports is likely to be tentative. Your chief of staff might be playing politics with a level of sophistication more than he or she is used to. He or she might not know when it's most useful to speak up or when it's more useful to stay in the background. In this context, you'll want to set expectations with your chief of staff and direct reports about the following things:

- What decisions he or she is authorized to make on your behalf
- When your staff can go straight to you and when they need to go through the chief of staff first
- What meetings the chief of staff should attend with you and which ones he or she should attend in your place
- Whether he or she has signing authority up to a certain monetary amount, partial or full P&L responsibility, and in what clearly defined areas
- The process for any unclear areas

For areas that are not defined, make explicit with your chief of staff and direct reports the probability of some trial and error, and then give your chief of staff permission to test the boundaries. You might need to do some repair work when your chief of staff oversteps his or her bounds. Still, nearly every executive I spoke with said they'd rather have a chief of staff who charged boldly ahead from the start and had to be "reined in" than one who was timid and had to be prompted to the right level of action. See "Identifying

Projects the Chief of Staff Can Own and Drive from Beginning to End," later in this chapter.

As part of your expectation setting, you can define the level to which your chief of staff should have a point of view on, and speak up about, various topics or participate in meetings. You can periodically call on him or her during a meeting to express a point of view. That point of view doesn't have to be the right one, per se, but it should be a thoughtful one. For one chief of staff, trust looked like this:

> I was in a meeting yesterday with a customer and my boss. I hadn't spoken a word in 45 minutes. I was following the conversation, and thankfully I resisted the urge to surf the Internet at certain points, because I was called upon to produce, from recollection, some numbers that were very important to the conversation. There's a certain ability to go from zero to business in an instant that's important in this role.

The executive in this situation expected the chief of staff to have those numbers, and he did. Without some prior expectation setting, that customer meeting could have gotten very awkward.

Once you have set the expectations, you begin the work of maintaining them. One president told me that her company's formerly hands-on founders hired her as president, in part, to prevent managers from "founder shopping" ideas and programs and going directly to one founder or another, effectively playing the founders and other managers off one another. "Similarly," she adds, "I have to ensure that my staff don't do that to me. It's not necessarily malicious—many of them are just used to doing things a certain way—but I always have to watch for it. They know what to come to me for and what to go to my chief of staff for. Sometimes my job is reminding them and reinforcing the expectations we set at the beginning."

You might need to consciously work on sending your direct reports back to the chief of staff before they come to you with certain types of questions or information, or making a habit of saying, "I want my chief of staff in the room for this discussion."

On the flip side, your chief of staff could lean too heavily on the weight of your office to accomplish your objectives instead of influencing the players and outcomes. Or he or she might feel enough pressure from this new position at the top of the organization to accomplish goals at any cost, even if it means manipulating people to get there. Largely, and somewhat counterintuitively, the chief of staff's success means not being demanding, using the weight of your office like a badge, or manipulating people.

In their book *Influence Without Authority*, authors Allan Cohen and David Bradford discuss the difference between influence and manipulation:

> Alternatively, some people desiring influence fake interest in the other person, go through the motions of making relationships, or are so instrumental in their approaches to others at every stage of attempting influence, that they are seen as manipulative, creating distrust in the process. No technique works well when the person using it is perceived as only self-interested.[1]

So your coaching the chief of staff to be genuine and honest is crucial to that person's long-term success—and yours. Being honest means admitting that he or she doesn't know all the answers and being transparent with others as much as possible. One chief of staff said that in the early going she used the phrase "Help me learn about this" ad nauseum. Amanda Mancuso at SCYNEXIS puts it this way: "My staff know that I'm here to help, I'm here to learn. I'm here to contribute to their objectives. You do that enough, people won't just trust you but they will see results." If people find one hidden agenda in you, they will always look for it after that, and you might not recover.

Yet full transparency at this level can require real courage; your chief of staff must be able to speak hard truth to you and others on staff who have vastly more experience, far more imposing titles, and very different compensation structures than he or she does. In fact, the chief of staff is often the only one who can—or will—speak the truth that this group needs to hear. Your chief of staff dances on a barbed-wire fence. On one side of the fence, the staff will look at how he or she pushes back on you as a sign that their viewpoints are being heard. On the other side of the fence, you are looking at how far the chief of staff carries your point of view in the face of opposition. One chief of staff put it this way:

> About 85 to 90 percent of the time I'm in the office, I'm not demanding something of anyone. I'm working with them. I've got my sleeves rolled up with them. Or I'm sitting at my desk and someone pops their head in, or I'm walking the halls. Making that time for those relationships is invaluable, especially for the 10 percent of the time that I have to demand something. If you spend a lot of your time coming across as rude, people won't think, "Oh, poor chief of staff, he's stressed out and has a tough job." They'll think, "What a jerk he is," and then when you come around, they're not going to want to help you.

In the early going, you'll want to monitor your staff to find out how the chief of staff is being received. You might even conduct an informal 360-degree review on your chief of staff through your HR partner to get feedback that people don't want to say to your face. You might be so used to discussing things with your staff without a chief of staff that the chief of staff loses key context for work that he or she is doing because you didn't share it. This situation can quickly devolve into people thinking that you're playing them off one another or manipulating them and can undermine people's trust in your leadership.

It's easy to see the value of setting expectations, but without your reinforcement of expectations on all sides, all the expectation setting in the world won't help.

## SEEKING OPPORTUNITIES TO BOND WITH YOUR CHIEF OF STAFF

At first, this heading might sound a little too touchy-feely for your comfort. Certainly, relationships have their inherent value, but I am not suggesting that you bond for the sake of bonding. Rather, I suggest you actively seek or create bonding opportunities because doing so affects the results you get from your chief of staff. Imagine trying to achieve that Radar O'Reilly–like quality of someone who understands your vision well enough to finish your sentence or actually play you in a meeting, without some kind of bonding.

Chances are, the early days of the job are the best time for this kind of experience. Your chief of staff is likely trying to outwork you and overinvest in time so that he or she can understand your world nearly as well as you do. Even if you're part of the 44 percent of executives who don't have previous experience with your chief of staff, it's not hard to find bonding experiences to expedite the trust-building process, but you might have to create them. Let the chief of staff shadow you in nearly every meeting for a few weeks. This is a popular and seemingly effective approach.

One chief of staff, who was hired from outside the geographic location and industry she landed in, traveled extensively with her executive at first to meet with investors, shadow him, and learn the business. Even though she took fewer trips with him over time, that initial time spent in an airplane, looking over materials, and discussing their upcoming meetings enabled them to build rapport and gave each of them insights into the other's way of thinking and reacting to different situations. She went as far as to say that it created their *dependence* on one another, where he provided high-level visionary thinking and she provided a systematic, detail-oriented approach to implementing his vision.

One chief of staff recalled how her executive often stayed late on a particular day of the week. So, the chief of staff began staying late, too, asking questions and showing how much she was learning.

## IDENTIFYING PROJECTS THE CHIEF OF STAFF CAN OWN AND DRIVE FROM BEGINNING TO END

In his book *Managing with Power*, author Jeffrey Pfeffer makes the following observation:

> [T]he power of position, and the use of that power, is more
> than just formal authority. It entails building and maintaining
> a reputation for being effective, and it entails the capacity to
> get things implemented. Without these two components, the
> power of formal positions tends to erode.[2]

Pfeffer's comments support an important point: the ability to
drive a project from beginning to end builds trust between your
office and the broader organization, which of course is critical to
your ability to use power effectively. Successfully implementing a
project builds trust by giving your chief of staff an opportunity
to establish credibility and competence with your direct reports
and other stakeholders in the organization, as a direct reflection on
you. It also gives the chief of staff short-term successes of his or her
own in a role that is mostly behind the scenes and mostly consists
of orchestrating the work of others. It therefore contributes to the
chief of staff's overall development and sets that person up for success beyond this role.

If your chief of staff is seen as incompetent, he or she can undermine people's perceptions of how *you* respect them. One HR executive recounted a time when the chief of staff failed to establish
trust with the executive's staff in terms of competence. "The staff
sometimes came to me, as their head of HR, with certain problems,
and when they had asked their executive a serious question, they
wondered why they got her 'lackey' in response." Ouch. Don't let
that be you.

One chief of staff for a high-tech company spent a fair amount
of his first two weeks ensuring that a day-long meeting with 30
Chinese delegates and some executives from a major aerospace
company went off without a hitch, ensuring that the right folks
were where they needed to be, presentation content was delivered in Chinese and English, and dinner and other logistics went
smoothly. He did all this while preparing himself and his executive for an upcoming board meeting, getting to know the team,
and learning the daily tasks and ongoing projects that he'd need to

attend to. He really wanted to show that he could deliver, and he simply put in as much time as needed to ensure the big event got done without a hiccup.

As part of giving the chief of staff ownership, you can, perhaps paradoxically, give him or her the space to make mistakes. Every chief of staff will have a "stumbling moment" early on in his or her tenure. In most cases, the chiefs of staff are taking on an incredible amount of work that they haven't done before in their careers. The likelihood of them encountering work that they didn't even know was their responsibility is high. On the other hand, they might encounter work that they thought was their responsibility but was actually shared with others; in such cases their unilateral action might be unappreciated by those who shared the responsibility and who don't like feeling cut out of the loop. Sometimes they might just carry their responsibilities too far. One chief of staff, in a moment that lived on in company lore, told an iconic, household-name company founder during a meeting to hurry up and make his point. The meeting was behind schedule, and the chief of staff—who had been told it was his job to keep the meeting running on time—was trying to be as diligent and as tactful as possible. After an awkward pause, the founder simply laughed and continued. The company's president pulled the chief of staff aside later and explained behind closed doors that he had overstepped his bounds. Whatever the "stumbling moment" may be, chiefs of staff have got to have a thick skin, to take the criticisms that will invariably be leveled at them, to make repairs where needed, and to continue the activity until they've got it right. These moments provide you with perhaps your best chance to act out your leadership brand, to help smooth over what needs smoothing, to take some of the chief of staff's heat, and to send a message to those around you regarding what happens to people in your organization who take thoughtful risks and are doing the best they can in a fast-moving environment.

Especially in the rotational version of the role, you are setting up this position—and the person in it—to shine. You want the chief of staff to be successful because it makes your job easier, reflects well on you, and because having a great experience makes it easier for that person to bring others into the role as you evolve it. Chiefs of staff report that one of their biggest challenges in the role is that from a career advancement or personal advancement point of view, they are essentially a shadow of the leader. The spotlight (and the seven-figure salaries) hits the leaders, not the chiefs of staff. One said, "If you are in the background, you don't get the credit; so what do you put on your resume? Many companies allocate bonuses and stock options based on peer-to-peer comparison, which isn't possible because one chief of staff isn't the same from one department to another, let alone one company to another or one industry to another. If you have a chief of staff who is compared with sales people, the sales people can point to more tangible dollar results, so managing your career as a chief of staff can be tricky."

Chiefs of staff can also get pigeonholed into staying in the role, and once they get labeled, they might have to leave the company to break out of the reputation of being a good runner-up leader. They need direct, tangible business achievements to point to so that they don't struggle with these issues and so that they stay motivated to perform their duties well. Giving them ownership is the most direct way to help.

Perhaps the best and most common area in which chiefs of staff drive projects from beginning to end is in cross-departmental work. See "Executing or Overseeing Work That Has No Clear Departmental Owner" in Chapter 3. See also "Special Projects" in Chapter 4 for examples of special projects that chiefs of staff in my interviews owned and drove.

Hopefully, it is now clear how your active involvement in the first 90 to 100 days can pay off.

## ◼ REFLECT & APPLY

After looking at the chief of staff's first 90 to 100 days, I offer the following questions for reflection and application:

1. Take a look at the three situations that started this chapter, and for each one, think what you'd do differently or how you'd manage the situation.

2. What expectations will be the most important for you to set with your chief of staff? Your staff? You won't know the answers to all of these questions until you hire someone, but this is a framework for getting started:
   - What decisions is the chief of staff authorized to make on your behalf?
   - When can your staff go straight to you and when do they need to go through the chief of staff first?
   - What meetings should the chief of staff attend *with* you and which ones should he or she attend *instead of* you?
   - Does your chief of staff have signing authority up to a certain monetary amount, partial or full P&L responsibility? How much, or in what areas?
   - What's the process that your chief of staff or staff should use for any unclear areas?

3. As you get close to hiring your chief of staff, look over your calendar for the next 90 days. What are some opportunities for bonding with your chief of staff?

   _____

   _____

   _____

4. Are there special projects on your horizon right now that could help your chief of staff establish credibility and trust with your staff? Use this space to jot down your ideas.

   _____

   _____

   _____

# 7

# Best Practices for
# Evolving the Role

As one chief of staff departs the role, you can take a fresh look at the concepts and reflections in Chapters 1 through 6. What has changed over the last two or three years in the organization dynamics, your leadership style or position, and the deliverables you are responsible for? Based on those answers, do you still need a chief of staff? If so, what should the emphasis be?

Chris Adams, in describing his experience as the "accidental long-term" chief of staff, indicated that in the beginning it took a senior leader (director level, VP) with a certain level of experience and sophistication to build relationships and bridges at the executive level, deal with tactical issues and specific problems that arose, and think strategically about how to implement standards, best practices, processes, communication, tempo, and business rhythms. After that, the job required a different level of experience and sophistication to sustain the existing structure. This approach might work better for companies in certain growth modes or stages of their lifecycles, which I covered in more depth in "Medium to

Large Size" in Chapter 2. It also might work better for leaders at the department or function level versus a CEO, as I discussed in "The leader's position" in Chapter 2. But this model of starting the role at a more senior level and then shifting to a more junior level is one that several of my interview respondents noted worked well.

The long-term or career chief of staff will rarely face the situation of having to re-enter the organization. At some point, however, your rotational chief of staff will, well, rotate. You can best support that chief of staff by helping determine the timing and substance of his or her next role, partnering in the reflection outlined in the first paragraph of this chapter, leaning on the chief of staff to find you some strong candidates for the next go-round, and helping him or her anticipate, and perhaps ease, re-entry challenges.

## DETERMINING THE TIMING AND SUBSTANCE OF YOUR CHIEF OF STAFF'S NEXT ROLE

The timing of most rotations seems to be about 24 to 36 months. However, the actual length might vary because of a number of factors:

- You're in the middle of an important strategic project in which continuity and completion trump the (somewhat arbitrary) 24-to-36-month guideline for rotation.
- The organizational dynamics, marketplace, or other factors have changed, such as in reorganizations in which you are the common, connecting thread between what's needed in the new organization and what worked and didn't in the old organization.
- You might find that there is no clear next step for your chief of staff in the organization as he or she approaches the end of your tenure. If this is the situation, you can just continue, or if you have a suitable replacement lined up already, you can bring the replacement in and, if there is a business need, keep the current chief of staff driving special projects for a while.

- A replacement for your current chief of staff is harder to find than anyone anticipated, and you might need to entice your chief of staff—who might be eager to find his or her next career move—to stay.

As I mentioned in "Identifying Projects the Chief of Staff Can Own and Drive from Beginning to End" in Chapter 6, you want your chief of staff to shine by landing well in his or her next role. It makes your job easier, reflects well on you, and makes it easier to recruit others into the role. Chiefs of staff often have a sense of where they want to go next, but most times they'll respect and at least listen to your suggestions. Your strongest role in this decision point can be partnering with your chief of staff to think about what has changed since day one in this role. He or she can use that reflection to help you think about the emphasis you need in the next chief of staff, and you can use it to help your chief of staff reflect on how far he or she has come developmentally, which can open up possibilities and lead to breakthrough thinking about what's next.

## FINDING YOUR CHIEF OF STAFF'S REPLACEMENT AND HANDING OFF

Certainly you'll rely on your HR team to source, interview, and hire your next chief of staff, but your current chief of staff is likely best suited for identifying other folks in the organization who could do the job. You will partner with your chief of staff to update the job description, conduct interviews, and hand off.

As Chris Adams noted about his transition out of the role, "The executive still needed the support, but it's a different type of support than when we assembled a new executive team and started fresh." When the staff was all new and learning to work together or with the executive, the chief of staff was very focused on some of the translational work mentioned previously in this chapter. Over time, the work became less focused on that kind of activity and more focused on deep-diving into the more intractable issues and bringing them to resolution. "When I left, it needed a more junior person with the ability to maintain an existing system more than a senior one to strategically set up the system."

As your thought partnership with your chief of staff leads to changes in the job description, your role becomes reviewer and approver of updates to that description. This activity can be a development area for the chief of staff in itself, because it might be the first time he or she has written a job description for a more complex situation than standard, clearly defined roles in his or her previous department or function, where templates are readily accessible.

One chief of staff for a colorful technology magnate with interests in all manner of humanitarian and science work talked about the challenge of figuring out exactly what his role was. He had been a chief of staff before, but the challenge was what it looked like *for this executive*. "My executive needed help with, well, just about all his interests," the chief of staff recalls. He just didn't know how to summarize it in a job description. Reflecting many of the executive's endeavors, the chief of staff job description was nebulous, vague, and poorly defined. It would have scared a lot of applicants away, and that would probably be good. Those looking for more definition weren't going to have it handed to them! His eventual chief of staff focused in his interviews with the executive on using managed ego and patience to figure out on a daily basis what would be needed. At one point in the interview, the chief of staff recalls, "I said, 'I want to make your life a little less annoying every day.'" To which his executive replied, "Perfect!"

Your role in interviewing should simply be to interview the strongest two or three candidates that your chief of staff, HR head, and any others in the interview loop have determined are ready for you. Ideally, the partnering you've done on the evolution of the role would reveal your top priorities and hot-button topics. In reality, these probably bubble up in your head while you're away from work. The beginning of the interview process is the best time to convey these.

In their book *You're in Charge—Now What?*, Thomas Neff and James Citrin cite the value of new CEOs meeting with their predecessors "for advice, training, contacts, and mentoring—even for making personal introductions to important clients, key shareholders, useful industry sources, and other constituents."[1] The chief of staff role is no different in that regard. You should plan to build in a reasonable handoff period, if possible. A couple weeks' overlap between one chief of staff and another tends to be ideal. And beware of too much overlap. Cut the cord quickly once those early connections are made. On the other hand, the business requirements and the reality of your situation might not allow for much handoff at all, much less an extended one. Here, you are back to "Setting and Reinforcing Expectations," as discussed in Chapter 6. The trick is to ensure that the organization knows whether the incoming or outgoing chief of staff is calling the shots, or which shots are being called by whom. You'll need to review your organization announcements and any other appropriate communications, which might also be drafted by the incoming or outgoing chief of staff in the first place.

You might request that your outgoing chief of staff create a handoff binder (electronic or print) with critical information that can serve as a reference whether or not there's a sufficient handoff. Things to include are useful information on your office—a quick detailing of the roles and responsibilities of the chief of staff and the executive assistant; a link to the company calendar; links to the most commonly used internal collaboration and team websites and distribution lists; emergency protocols; staff and staff EA contact lists; routines around executive leadership and board meetings, the company's strategic-planning process, and annual performance-management processes; and personal details about the executive, such as food and travel preferences.

## HELPING THE CHIEF OF STAFF COPE WITH RE-ENTRY CHALLENGES

At some point, your outgoing chief of staff is ready to "re-enter" a functional leadership role in the organization. Re-entry might imply that he or she somehow left the organization and is returning, but I have chosen the term more because it reflects the sense in which the chief of staff is taken out of a functional job, is placed in a position where he or she can see and participate in what happens across the entire business, and then returns to a particular function.

Upon arriving at their new destinations, chiefs of staff start running up against ways of being or acting that worked in the chief of staff role but won't work in their new world. In performance conversations or one-on-one meetings with the outgoing chief of staff, you can help him or her anticipate—and in some situations ease— re-entry challenges.

One chief of staff found his challenge was having direct reports again. "As a chief of staff, you often don't have direct reports. You have more flexibility to change your priorities. Now you've got others dependent on you, so that if you change, they must change, too. When your decision to change has so many ripple effects, it creates a higher standard for when you change direction."

Another chief of staff landed in an investor relations role after her stint. She found that reintegrating with a functional or departmental team posed unexpected challenges. "As chief of staff, you *were* the team. In some ways you become self-reliant in that role, and that can get in your way when you get placed back in the organization."

Another challenge for outgoing chiefs of staff who are re-entering the organization can be balancing their new, broader perspective with their new responsibility for a departmental point of view. One chief of staff talked about the complexity of her transition out of the COS role, where she still had one foot in the chief of staff role and one foot in a new management position: "I previously managed mostly at the macro level. I occasionally dove into the details as needed but tried to pull in the right individuals to handle the tactics. Comparatively, my new management role seems very focused on the micro level of managing my own business. While I think I've been fairly successful at beginning to transition my thought patterns, it's been a challenge to try to bounce back and forth between the two. Though having the macro perspective obviously has benefit at the micro level, I find I can either focus on the major impacts to the entire production system, or on the details of my little slice of it. When I attempt to have a firm grasp on both, one or the other suffers."

One former chief of staff had developed an instinct and reaction to operational issues that no longer served him when he became a director of business development. "I'd be sitting in a meeting with my new team's leadership and, upon hearing a challenge that they were working through, would find myself following up with people to find out if I could help them resolve the (often cross-department) challenges. While some of that work was tangentially related to my new business development role, much of it was not at all related, and any effort I spent helping others with their operating challenges would take me away from my new focus and tasks, and it risked alienating those on the leadership team who were tasked with handling operations. I had to temper that generalist attitude and instinct."

Nearly every chief of staff I interviewed who had gone through a re-entry process noted that being removed from the seat of power was a challenge. The former chief of staff has to relearn how to lead from his or her own authority again versus yours. Also, tapping into the flow of information or knowing what's really going on in the organization is harder than when the former chief of staff was at the top. Further, many reported that, at least in the early going after leaving the chief of staff role, their time was wasted by people trying to get information that they no longer had. It was as though everyone suddenly became an investigative journalist, trying to get the exclusive story on what's really going on at the top. They expected the outgoing chief of staff to know what's going on because that person *was* in that position. However, reality changes pretty quickly; the outgoing chief of staff probably doesn't know much after a couple weeks, even if confidentiality protocols enabled him or her to share the information. It doesn't hurt for the outgoing chief of staff to have a scripted response to inquiries like this and to learn to say no.

There might be other re-entry challenges, but the important thing for the re-entering chief of staff to remember is to make time during the transition to reflect on what is going to be different in the new world.

## EXAMPLES OF EVOLUTIONS

One chief of staff who experienced the role during his company's transition from small (a couple dozen employees) to mid-size (several hundred employees), described the evolution of the role this way:

> When I came into the role, the job was building a house of operations at the enterprise level. I had to clear the lot, put in a foundation, and install plumbing for that house. That included setting up governance frameworks and processes, communication channels, and RACI matrices. This transition was particularly tumultuous. In one year we replaced our head of HR, general counsel, and CFO. In addition to laying the foundation, I was focused on teambuilding and spec'ing new hires' job descriptions for the way my boss and I envisioned the organization. When I handed the role off to my successor, it was mostly about helping the boss develop her agenda, make sure the agenda and right priorities were being executed, and helping with air traffic control, which—in addition to day-to-day operations—meant managing a list of special projects on her plate, including:
>
> - A revamp of executive compensation packages
> - Several frameworks for new business models or determining which business models we'd move forward with
> - A revamp of our planning and budgeting process
> - A comprehensive business review of some of our core functions
>
> There were new special projects coming online, too. The new chief of staff was going to have to drive more programmatic involvement between groups, to make sure we used our collective strengths while maintaining the autonomy of the

core functions. That work was in the context of an increasing focus on return for investors and cost cutting.

Another chief of staff, working in Asia and Europe for a major consulting company, was lured by a Fortune 100 computer hardware company in the United States:

> They called and said, "Can you come to the U.S. and play a chief of staff role for a new group we're setting up to look at strategy and acquisitions?" The team was about 60–70 people with a $12 million budget. I would be helping them with strategy formulation and how that translates into revenue generation over the next three years or more, as well as the operations needed to get there. It takes an operational cadence to get right the business intelligence, market intelligence, budget management, and headcount; ensure we're taking on the right projects; and review talent against those projects. My job was largely making sure execs, their chiefs of staff (there were multiple in this organization), and planning and strategy leads are aligned. I had to have an awareness of where people were in their careers, where their skills and ambitions lie, and the organizational politics, advising the executive on the things happening or needing to happen for us as a group—and their overall boss—to be successful.
>
> Over time, as the role evolves to more of an operational maintenance mode, I'm moving on, trying to find another group where I can be a part of creating something new and help to scale it. I want to see connections happen and bring them together. If they're already mostly working together, it's a different role and far less fulfilling for me.

## ■ REFLECT & APPLY

After you've had a chance to think about your current chief of staff's tenure, I offer the following questions for reflection and application:

1. What changes have you noticed in the organization dynamics, benefits that you might receive from the chief of staff, importance or quality of deliverables that you're responsible for, or emphasis that you need?

   *Organization dynamics:*
   Changes: _____

   Continue chief of staff role?   ☐ Yes   ☐ No
   If yes, what changes in emphasis are suggested?

   _____

   *Benefits you might receive from the chief of staff:*
   Changes: _____

   Continue chief of staff role?   ☐ Yes   ☐ No
   If yes, what changes in emphasis are suggested?

   _____

   *Importance or quality of deliverables you're responsible for:*
   Changes: _____

   Continue chief of staff role?   ☐ Yes   ☐ No
   If yes, what changes in emphasis are suggested?

   _____

   *Emphasis:*
   Changes: _____

   Continue chief of staff role?   ☐ Yes   ☐ No
   If yes, what changes in emphasis are suggested?

   _____

   _____

*Other relevant areas:*
Changes: _____

Continue chief of staff role?   ☐ Yes   ☐ No
If yes, what changes in emphasis are suggested?

_____

_____

2. What attributes of your current chief of staff do you want to keep in the incoming chief of staff? Which ones do you want to let go of? Based on what's changed, what are some new opportunities that the incoming chief of staff can help with?

Attributes to keep: _____

_____

_____

_____

Attributes to let go of: _____

_____

_____

_____

New opportunities: _____

_____

_____

_____

3. Based on what you know of your chief of staff's strengths, what kind of role would help him or her excel? Use this as the basis for an engagement or professional development conversation with your outgoing chief of staff.

_____

_____

_____

_____

# EPILOGUE

As I've shown, being a leader in today's business environment is as complicated as ever. You can't succeed on your own, and a chief of staff can make a great addition to your team. I hope that through the various pivots, issues, and questions in this book, I've provided not a one-size-fits-all formula or answers that presume that I know you or your organization but rather the context in which you can decide if a chief of staff makes sense for you and your organization.

We all have defining moments in our lives, those times when a high-stakes choice must be made and the outcome from the choice will not be trivial. I asked each leader in my interviews (whether chief of staff, C-suite executive, or HR executive) for the "situation room" story—a big decision to be made or a crisis to be averted, an opportunity that put the chief of staff in a unique position to shine. I got a few good examples in return: a corporate chief of staff who had previously served as a government chief of staff in the U.S. Department of the Interior during the Deep Water Horizon disaster, the chief of staff I mentioned in Chapter 2 who found her executive and corporate team a couple blocks away from a bomb blast during a business trip, and several weighty decisions that affected the strategic direction of companies.

Most of life, however, is lived in the realm of mundane, day-to-day decisions and interactions in our personal life and our work. Whether or not my interview respondents had compelling, dramatic stories like the few I mentioned, they all made it clear that it's in the everyday decisions that the chief of staff adds value. The value of the role and the people who fill it is in the work most people never know about.

# NOTES

## Introduction—The $50 Million Question

1. Beth Kowitt with Alyssa Abkowitz, "Latest CEO Accessory: A Chief of Staff," *Fortune* (January 20, 2010): http://money.cnn.com/2010/01/19/news/companies/ceo_chief_of_staff.fortune/index.htm
2. Brooke Sopelsa, "Chiefs of Staff Make Their Way to Corporate America," CNBC (January 7, 2011): http://www.cnbc.com/id/40967945
3. Jon Picoult, "Check with My Chief of Staff," *Wall Street Journal* (December 31, 2010): http://online.wsj.com/articles/SB10001424052970203513204576048081165174642.
4. Al Chase, *Chief of Staff—A Force Multiplier!* White Rhino Report (Cambridge, MA, 2007): http://whiterhinoreport.blogspot.com/2007/02/chief-of-staff-white-paper-back-by.html

## Chapter 1—Definition, History, and Corporate Context of the Chief of Staff Role

1. Yoshitaro Takenobu, *The Japan Yearbook; Complete Cyclopaedia of General Information and Statistics on Japan and Japanese Territories* (Tokyo: Japan Year Book Office, 1928); Ian Neary, *Leaders & Leadership in Japan* (Japan Library/Curzon Press, Ltd., 1996), 137.
2. Philippe de Courcillon (Marq. de Dangeau), *Memoirs of the Court of France from 1684–1720*, Tr. by J. Davenport from the *Diary of the Marquis de Dangeau with Notes* (Nabu Press, 2012).
3. A. J. Pollard, *Warwick the Kingmaker* (London: Hambledon, 2007).
4. Peter Berglar, *Thomas More: A Lonely Voice Against the Power of the State* (New York: Scepter Publishers, 2009); Tracy Borman, *Thomas Cromwell: The Untold Story of Henry VIII's Most Faithful Servant* (London: Hodder & Stoughton, 2014); Robert Hutchinson, *Thomas Cromwell: The Rise and Fall of Henry VIII's Most Notorious Minister* (London: Phoenix, 2008).
5. General Count Philip de Ségur, *Memoirs of an Aide-de-Camp of Napoleon 1800–1812*, Tr. H.A. Patchett-Martin (Nonsuch Publishing, 2005).
6. Peter Wetzler, *Hirohito and War: Imperial Tradition and Military Decision Making in Pre-War Japan* (Honolulu: University of Hawaii Press, 1998).
7. http://www.guideposts.org/personal-growth/betrayed-ceo-finds-forgiveness-faith

8. Chase, *Force Multiplier*.
9. Paul Douglas Lockhart, *The Drillmaster of Valley Forge: The Baron de Steuben and the Making of the American Army* (New York: Harper Collins, 2008).
10. http://millercenter.org/academic/americanpresident/policy/whitehouse
11. "Capitalizing on Complexity": http://www-935.ibm.com/services/us/ceo/ceostudy2010/index.html
12. Thomas J. Neff and James M. Citrin, *You're In Charge—Now What?* (New York: Three Rivers Press, 2005).
13. Duncan Norton-Taylor, "How Top Executives Live (*Fortune* 1955)," *Fortune* (May 6, 2012): http://features.blogs.fortune.cnn.com/2012/05/06/classic-top-500-executives/
14. Alfred P. Sloan, Jr., *My Years with General Motors*. (New York: Doubleday, 1963).
15. Henrietta Brooks, Denver Barrows, Hedy Chen, Stas Kiianchenko, Cadet Steven Lee, Malik Neal, Anne-Sophie Schratz, and Cadet El Cook, *The Global Economy*; Senior Advisor Ken Chenault; *The New York Times* (2015): http://nytimesinleadership.com/spotlight/the-global-economy/
16. Timothy S. Breene, Paul F. Nunes, and Walter E. Shill, "The Chief Strategy Officer," *Harvard Business Review* (October 2007): http://hbr.org/2007/10/the-chief-strategy-officer/ar/1; Paul Hagen, "The Rise of the Chief Customer Officer," HBR Blog Network, Harvard Business Press): http://blogs.hbr.org/cs/2011/04/the_rise_of_the_chief_customer.html; Jeff Smisek, "Adapting to Ever-Changing Challenges," Stanford Graduate School of Business (April 1, 2011): http://www.gsb.stanford.edu/news/headlines/VFTT_smisek_2011.html
17. Boris Groysberg, L. Kevin Kelly, and Bryan MacDonald, "The New Path to the C-Suite," *Harvard Business Review* (March 2011). http://hbr.org/2011/03/the-new-path-to-the-c-suite/ar/1
18. Brett Thomas, *Leadership Manifesto*: http://integralleadershipmanifesto.com/manifesto/the-problem-with-leadership-theory/
19. Douglas Riddle, *Senior Leadership Team Coaching: A Center for Creative Leadership White Paper* (2008): http://www.ccl.org/leadership/pdf/research/SeniorLeadTeamCoaching.pdf
20. Chuck Lucier, Rob Schuyt, and Junichi Handa, "CEO Succession 2003—The Perils of Good Governance," Booz Allen Hamilton (2003); Margarethe Wiersema, "Crisis in the Boardroom: Lessons from CEO Dismissals," White Paper (Irvine, CA: Graduate School of Management, University of California, Irvine, 2002).

## Chapter 2—Organization Dynamics That Justify a Chief of Staff

1. Melissa Wingard-Phillips, *Why More Startups Should Consider Adding a Chief of Staff to Support the CEO*, Whiterhinoreport.blogspot.com (Oct. 7, 2013): http://whiterhinoreport.blogspot.com/2013/10/why-more-startups-should-consider.html

2. These statistics were derived from a variety of sources, including Fortune 500 (http://fortune.com/fortune500/), LinkedIn, and Yahoo! Finance, as well as individual company financial reports, investor reports, and summaries where available.

3. Wingard-Phillips, *Why More Startups*.

4. Wingard-Phillips, *Why More Startups*.

5. Dan Marlin, Bruce T. Lamont, and Scott W. Geiger, "Diversification Strategy and Top Management Team Fit," *Journal of Managerial Issues* (Fall 2004)

6. Jamie Grierson, "RBS to Sell Off Churchill and Direct Line Insurance Arm (September 14, 2012): http://www.independent.co.uk/news/business/news/rbs-to-sell-off-churchill-and-direct-line-insurance-arm-8138751.html

7. Alec Mattinson, "Direct Line Director of Comms Rob Bailhache Leaves Following RBS Spin-Off," *PR Week* (March 4, 2014): http://www.prweek.com/article/1283203/direct-line-director-comms-rob-bailhache-leaves-following-rbs-spin-off

8. Angelica Mari, "CIO Interview: Angela Morrison, Chief Information Officer, Direct Line," *ComputerWeekly*.com (November 6, 2013): http://www.computerweekly.com/news/2240208561/CIO-interview-Angela-Morrison-chief-information-officer-Direct-Line

9. David Ulrich and Norm Smallwood, "Capitalizing on Capabilities," *Harvard Business Review* (June 2004): https://hbr.org/2004/06/capitalizing-on-capabilities

10. Michael Wade, "Organizational Complexity: The Hidden Killer" (November 2013): http://www.imd.org/research/challenges/TC084-13-organizational-complexity-michael-wade.cfm.

11. Julian Brinkshaw and Suzanne Heywood, "Putting Organizational Complexity in Its Place," McKinsey Insights and Publications (May 2010): http://www.mckinsey.com/insights/organization/putting_organizational_complexity_in_its_place; Tony Schwartz and Christine Porath, "Why You Hate Work," *The New York Times Sunday Review* (May 30, 2014): http://www.nytimes.com/2014/06/01/opinion/sunday/why-you-hate-work.html?_r=0

12. Chris Wells, "What's Keeping CEOs Up at Night? Six Facts That Will Surprise You," Kapta Systems (April 8, 2014): http://www.kaptasystems.com/resources/what-keeps-ceos-up-at-night-six-facts-that-will-surprise-you/

13. Kurt Lewin, Ronald Lippit, and Ralph K. White, "Patterns of Aggressive Behavior in Experimentally Created Social Climates," *Journal of Social Psychology*, 10, 271–301 (1939); Robert R. Blake and Anne Adams McCanse, *Leadership Dilemmas- Grid® Solutions: A Visionary New Look at a Classic Tool for Defining and Attaining Leadership and Management Excellence (Blake/Mouton Grid Management & Organization Development)*, (Gulf

Professional Publishing, 1991); Richard Boyatzis and Annie McKee, *Resonant Leadership: Renewing Yourself and Connecting with Others Through Mindfulness, Hope, and Compassion* (Boston: Harvard Business School Press, 2005); Eric Flamholtz and Yvonne Randle, *Growing Pains: Transitioning from an Entrepreneurship to a Professionally Managed Firm* (San Francisco: Jossey-Bass, 2007); James McGregor Burns, *Leadership* (1st Ed.) (New York: Harper Perennial Modern Classics, 2010).

## Chapter 3—Reported Benefits of the Chief of Staff Role

1. Les Trachtman, "CEOs Must Find Time for Strategic Planning: Here's How to Do It," *The Washington Post: On Small Business* (March 23, 2012): http://www.washingtonpost.com/business/on-small-business/ceos-must-find-time-for-strategic-planning—heres-how-to-do-it/2012/03/20/gIQAdnQrVS_story.html.
2. Michael E. Porter, Jay W. Lorsch, and Nitin Nohria, "The Seven Things That Surprise New CEOs," Harvard Business School (October 20, 2008). http://hbswk.hbs.edu/item/6039.html
3. Ernest Hemingway, *A Farewell to Arms* (New York: Scribner, 1957), 147.
4. "Chief Receptionist Officer? Title Inflation Hits the C-Suite," Knowledge @ Wharton (May 30, 2007): http://knowledge.wharton.upenn.edu/article/chief-receptionist-officer-title-inflation-hits-the-c-suite/; Bill Taylor, "Does Your Job Title Get the Job Done?" *Harvard Business Review* (July 15, 2010): https://hbr.org/2010/07/does-your-job-title-get-the-jo
5. Timothy S. Breene, Paul F. Nunes, and Walter E. Shill, "The Chief Strategy Officer, *Harvard Business Review* (October 2007): http://hbr.org/2007/10/the-chief-strategy-officer/ar/1; Paul Hagen, "The Rise of the Chief Customer Officer," HBR Blog Network (April 18, 2011): http://blogs.hbr.org/cs/2011/04/the_rise_of_the_chief_customer.html
6. Thomas J. Saporito, "It's Time to Acknowledge CEO Loneliness," HBR Blog Network (February 15, 2012): http://blogs.hbr.org/2012/02/its-time-to-acknowledge-ceo-lo/
7. Chris Wells, "What's Keeping CEOs Up at Night? Six Facts That Will Surprise You," Kapta Systems (April 8, 2014): http://www.kaptasystems.com/resources/what-keeps-ceos-up-at-night-six-facts-that-will-surprise-you/
8. Porter, Lorsch, and Nohria, "The Seven Things."
9. "Enron Officials: We Didn't Know," *USA Today* (February 7, 2002): http://usatoday30.usatoday.com/money/energy/enron/2002-02-08-hearings.htm
10. Robert A. Heinlein, *Stranger in a Strange Land* (New York: Berkley, 1961).
11. S. Moscovici and M. Zavalloni, "The Group as a Polarizer of Attitudes," *Journal of Personality and Social Psychology* 12, no. 2 (1969): 125–135, DOI:10.1037/h0027568; D. R. Forsyth, *Group Dynamics*, 5th ed. (Pacific Grove, CA: Brooks/Cole, 2009).
12. A. Hermann and H. G. Rammal, "The Grounding of the 'Flying Bank,'"

*Management Decision* 48, no. 7 (2010): 1051, doi:10.1108/
00251741011068761; Jack Eaton, "Management Communication: The
Threat of Groupthink," *Corporate Communication*, 6 (2001): 183–192;
Allison McQueen, "A Groupthink Perspective on the Invasion of Iraq,"
*International Affairs Review* 14, no. 2 (Fall 2005); Emma Rowley, "IMF
'Groupthink' Masked the Dangers of Financial Crisis, Finds Watchdog,"
*The Telegraph*: http://www.telegraph.co.uk/finance/economics/8314688/
IMF-groupthink-masked-dangers-of-financial-crisis-finds-watchdog
.html; Gillian Tett, "Lost Through Destructive Creation," *Financial
Times/*FT.com (March 9, 2009); Roland Benabou, "Groupthink: Collec-
tive Delusions in Organizations and Markets," *The Review of Economic
Studies* (September 17, 2012): doi: 10.1093/restud/rds030

13. Panetta, "The President's Gatekeepers."
14. Sir Martin Sorrell, Randy Komisar, and Anne Mulcahy; Olivier Sibony
    and Allen Webb, editors. "How We Do It: Three Executives Reflect on
    Strategic Decision Making," *McKinsey Quarterly* (March 2010): http://
    www.mckinsey.com/insights/strategy/how_we_do_it_three_executives
    _reflect_on_strategic_decision_making
15. Dan Ariely, *Are We in Control of Our Own Decisions*? TED (December
    2008): http://www.ted.com/talks/dan_ariely_asks_are_we_in_control_
    of_our_own_decisions; Robert A. Burton, *On Being Certain: Believing
    You Are Right Even When You're Not* (New York: St Martins, 2008).
    J. Luft and H. Ingham, "The Johari Window: A Graphic Model of Inter-
    personal Awareness," Proceedings of the Western Training Laboratory
    in Ggroup Development (Los Angeles: UCLA, 1955); Joseph Luft, *Of
    Human Interaction* (Palo Alto, CA: National Press, 1969): 177.
16. Liz Wiseman, *Multipliers* (New York: Harper Collins, 2010).
17. Panetta, "The President's Gatekeepers."
18. Rick Maurer, *Beyond the Wall of Resistance: Why 70% of All Changes Still
    Fail—And What You Can Do About It* (Austin, TX: Bard Press, 2010).
19. Dibeyendu Ganguly, "The Outsider: Why Companies Take Risk of Hiring
    CEOs with No Industry Experience," *The Economic Times* (October 25,
    2013): http://articles.economictimes.indiatimes.com/2013-10-25/news/
    43366964_1_banking-services-experience-air-asia-india; Christopher
    Gearon, "Wanted: Hospital CEOs Without Healthcare Experience," *US
    News & World Reports* (January 28, 2014): http://health.usnews.com/
    health-news/hospital-of-tomorrow/articles/2014/01/28/wanted-
    hospital-ceos-without-health-care-experience; Ayse Karaevli and
    Edward J. Zajac, "When Is an Outsider CEO a Good Choice?" *MIT
    Sloan Management Review* (Summer 2012): http://sloanreview.mit.edu/
    article/when-is-an-outsider-ceo-a-good-choice/
20. Research conducted by Seattle University team of William Maroon
    and Jennifer Yu, under direction of Peter Raven, analyzing the career

progressions of more than 500 corporate chiefs of staff on LinkedIn.

21. Dinah Wisenberg Brin, "Why You Should Hire for Potential, Not for Experience," *Fast Company* (September 22, 2014): http://www .fastcompany.com/3035990/hit-the-ground-running/why-you-should- hire-for-potential-not-experience; Joe Santana, "Hire Talent and Passion over Skill and Experience," *Tech Republic* (November 11, 2002): http:// www.techrepublic.com/article/hire-talent-and-passion-over-skill-and- experience/; Marcus Buckingham and Curt Coffman, *First, Break All The Rules: What the World's Greatest Managers Do Differently* (New York: Simon and Schuster, 1999).

22. Theresa Minton-Eversole, "Concerns Grow over Workforce Retirements and Skills Gaps," *SHRM HR Topics & Strategy, Staffing Management Articles* (April 9, 2012): http://www.shrm.org/hrdisciplines/staffingmanagement/ articles/pages/workforceretirementandskillgaps.aspx; Brandon Rigoni and Amy Adkins, "As Baby Boomers Retire, It's Time to Replenish Talent," *Gallup Business Journal* (January 28, 2015): http://www.gallup.com/ businessjournal/181295/baby-boomers-retire-time-replenish-talent.aspx; "Effective Knowledge Transfer Can Help Transform Your Bottom Line," American Management Association (August 5, 2010): http://www .amanet.org/training/articles/Effective-Knowledge-Transfer-Can- Help-Transform-Your-Bottom-Line.aspx; Stephanie Armour, "Who Wants to Be a Middle Manager?" *USA Today* (August 13, 2007): http:// usatoday30.usatoday.com/money/workplace/2007-08-12-no- manage_N.htm?AID=4011243&PID=3662453&SID=skim725X329128 X6b791b41fa83949dd6b29d9fb9d7ae19

### Chapter 5—Finding and Hiring the Right Candidates

1. Career progression data from Payscale.com, LinkedIn.

2. Edward Jung, internal memo on hiring a technical assistant. Used with permission.

3. Combined averages from research at Salary.com, Payscale.com, and the U.S. Bureau of Labor and Statistics, using various search parameters.

4. *The Devil Wears Prada*, Twentieth Century Fox (2006).

5. Chase, *Force Multiplier*.

6. Viveat Susan Pinto, "The Lady Who Knows What's Brewing at Tata Star- bucks," *Business Standard* (September 29, 2012): http://www.business- standard.com/article/companies/the-lady-who-knows-what-s-brewing- at-tata-starbucks-112092900054_1.html

7. Chase, *Force Multiplier*.

### Chapter 6—Expectations for the First 90–100 Days

1. Allan R. Cohen and David L. Bradford, *Influence Without Authority*, 2nd ed. (Hoboken, NJ: Wiley & Sons, 2005): 31.

2. Jeffrey Pfeffer, *Managing with Power: Politics and Influence in Organizations* (Boston: Harvard Business Press, 1992): 128.

## Chapter 7—Best Practices for Evolving the Role

1. Thomas J. Neff and James M. Citrin, *You're in Charge—Now What?* (New York: Crown, 2005): 26.

CPSIA information can be obtained
at www.ICGtesting.com
Printed in the USA
LVHW081109070323
741091LV00002B/3